"Tom Wood reminds us once again that grace is vital, not optional. God's grace draws us like an oasis in the desert, quenching our thirst and making us thirsty for more. Tom embodies this gospel-centered grace in his teaching, his discipleship, and his writing. *Vital Grace* will make you smile as you are reminded once again of the Giver of this lavish gift—Jesus Christ our Lord."

DOUG SAUDER

Lead pastor, Calvary Chapel, Ft. Lauderdale, Florida

"Vital Grace is like a defibrillator awakening us to experience a radical outpouring of God's grace. My heart's tendency to cling to pharisaical righteousness needs the gospel. I need to be saved every day from my guilt and shame. Rather than living as futile performers, we are to lead a lifestyle of grace. This book is a must for both Christians and non-Christians"

REV. DR. BILL SIM

Korean ministries coordinator, Mission to North America, PCA

"This book offers a refreshing reminder of the real freedom Christ purchased on our behalf. *Vital Grace* will help you flourish and not flounder as you better understand and walk in God's free grace. Tom gives engaging illustrations and explains the gospel in 3D in a way that will resonate with you. I encourage you to read this book and to apply the biblical principles. You will not regret it."

DR. RAY GENTRY

President/CEO, Southern Baptist Conference of Associational Leaders (SBCAL)

"With a pastor's heart and tone, Dr. Tom Wood penetrates a cultural atmosphere in which the grace of God is too often misunderstood, twisted, and even abused. *Vital Grace* unfolds the mystery and majesty of grace and truth, and is laced with the practical wisdom of a seasoned leader. The result is a timely resource that has the potential to transform anyone who wishes to lead others—and be led—into the deeper riches of God's vital grace."

KAREN A. ELLIS

Director, The Edmiston Center for the Study of the Bible and Ethnicity

"Dr. Wood has written a timely book that drives right at the heart of our Christian lives and the motivation of the Christian's walk with the Lord. In an upside-down world, he points us back to the vitality of grace, reminding us that grace is not only the mechanism by which we are saved, but grace is also the engine of the Christian life. My heart bursts with thanksgiving at the much-needed reminder!"

DR. IKE REEDER

President, Birmingham Theological Seminary

"Soak your soul in the gospel truth of *Vital Grace*. In this wonderful new book, Tom Wood helps us go deep in understanding who we are and the idols we cherish. He then shows us how to apply the truths of vital grace so we don't just believe the gospel but live it in ways that transform our lives and ministries."

REV. RALPH CUNNINGTON

Pastor, City Church Manchester, United Kingdom

"Dr. Tom Wood has given us a gift in *Vital Grace*. His unflinching look at our current challenges in light of a hope that our culture can't give kept me turning each page. This book is a winner and needs to be read by anyone who is serious about going deeper in their walk with Christ."

REV. DAVID WHITEHEAD

Senior director, City To City, Global; author of *Making Sense of the Bible*

"Mining deep and precious veins of Scripture, Tom Wood draws a multi-faceted picture of grace. Using powerful testimony and illustration, he proves that grace is not a one-dimensional ointment that soothes us in our sin, but rather a rich and many-splendored grace that emerges from the holy love of God in Christ. Real grace is costly, always moving us to repentance and propelling us into a life of consecrated discipleship."

REV. JOHN SMED

Author of *Prayer Revolution*; founding director, Prayer Current

Vital GRACE

GETTING EVERYTHING FOR NOTHING

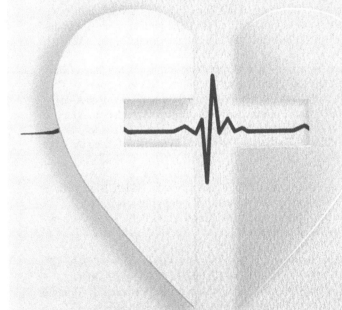

TOM WOOD

CO-AUTHOR OF GOSPEL COACH

ISBN: 978-0-9890758-8-6

Contents

Acknowledgments

No one gets Vital Grace on their own. Obviously, God the Holy Spirit is the first Cause of grace in life, however, God's method of forming His people by grace is His people, as a second cause. Over my life, I have received grace by mentors, teachers, friends, and colleagues who have taught me, both in word and by life, what Vital grace is, so I want to thank just a few of them!

Dr. Steve Brown deeply infected me with grace and has, for over 40 years, dispensed grace in his teaching and in our personal friendship. My wife and daughters thank him as well!

Dr. Bill Crabb gave me a paradigm and instructed me in grace application some 35 plus years ago. He experienced "full glory" many years ago, but he had such influence during our short friendship.

Steven Curtis Chapman, who through our mutual friend with Scotty Smith, I've only met twice, has taught me much of God's grace through his music and story.

Dr. J. Allen Thompson, a man of great humility and wise spirituality, has spent hours of his life guiding, teaching, loving, encouraging, and investing in my life. I have been changed by his friendship.

My colleague and friend Jim Moon Jr. is a man of many talents, is an exceptional Gospel coach and trainer.

John Smed, a friend who is "closer than a brother" and with whom I have spent the past 25 years discussing, arguing and praying the gospel together.

Thanks to the many friends who have made significant support over the years to the mission of CMM, Inc., that now has a global footprint of gospel influence. I would not have been able to do all we've been a part of without their friendship.

Thank you, Rick and Barb, Shaun and Kathy, Greg and Debra, Kris and Cindy, Gary and Barbara, Samuel and Sarah, Mike and Sherrie, Rich and Donna, Lee and Ginny, Rick and Pam, Humberto and Shannon, Lundy and Kit, Clark and Martha, Allen and Cecilia, Stan and Lori, John and Jeann, Lee, Bryan, Eddie, Mike, Zach, Michael, Mark, Erik, Steve, Tim, Jane, Cecilia, Carlos, Robert, Jack, Corb, Ed, Jim, and the many businesses, charitable foundations and churches that have partnered with me these many years. You have excelled in the grace of giving and demonstrated a character of generosity so that all over the world the gospel is growing and multiplying.

Ms. Amy Stevens, talented manager of a global ministry and "queen bee."

To Rachel, my closest friend in this renewal-needy world, who shows me what grace is every day.

Major thanks to Ms. Julie Carter, a skilled writer herself, who handled the production, copy, book, and cover layout. Everything I write passes through her.

Ms. Ginger Kolbaba, whose editing gift made this a much better book then when it started.

ONE

The Vitality of Grace

Grace is a word of central importance—the keyword of Christianity.

J. I. Packer

I am a *lifer*. In the military that would mean I had chosen a career to serve and protect the life and liberty of my countrymen. If I were a convict, it would mean I had been sentenced to live the rest of my life in prison. But I mean that I have spent my entire life in church. I was born into a "churched" family in which my parents were interested in my siblings and me getting a good Christian upbringing. Most of my life as a Christian has been based on God's grace, but that was not always the case.

Every Sunday as I was growing up, we attended Sunday school and church services. Usually our summers included vacation Bible school, Christian camp, backyard Bible clubs, or other serious church events. I was singing "This Little Light of Mine" long before I even had a little light. We learned the stories of Adam and Eve eating the apple; baby Moses lying in the basket; the Israelites crossing the Red Sea; David slaying Goliath; Daniel being thrown in the lion's den; Jonah getting swallowed by a whale; Jesus feeding the five thousand; and Jesus walking on water.

As I grew older, I went to a Christian high school and had a Bible class every week. I memorized Bible verses, outlines, and themes. We learned that the Bible had sixty-six books (thirty-nine in the Old Testament and twenty-seven in the New) and had been written over more than fourteen hundred years, on three different continents, by more than forty different authors, and in at least three different languages.

Eventually, I graduated from a Christian college where I studied the Bible more in depth. Like I said, I am a *lifer*.

Yet the aim in all those years seemed to be to make me into a "good boy" and one day a morally upright person. I was to work hard to be an obedient son, a nice date, a well-behaved citizen, a servant leader, and eventually a loving husband and good dad. Bible studies I attended were essentially moral lessons for structuring life. Sermons were moral lessons from the Bible with strategies on managing sin.

Although I do not remember anyone saying it exactly this way, the message I "heard" was, *You are a sinner, so accept Jesus as your Savior. Once you do, you have to try hard to obey God's ways because you don't want to make God unhappy.* In fact, the only way to have a blessed and happy life was to try hard to obey the commands God had for us. We were to "trust and obey, for there's no other way to be happy in Jesus."[1]

In my early twenties, even though I had the words of grace and knew about the grace of God, I began to hear the beautiful sounds in the music of God's free grace. A grace movement began in my heart, and that grace became the antidote to living a morally restrained life in true spirituality. Grace was not a "counter balance" to the rules. It was not an invitation to be free from rules, but it did make me free. Free to enjoy life with God.

The music came to me through writers such as Francis Schaeffer, Steve Brown, J. I. Packer, Chuck Swindoll, Jack Miller, and Philip Yancey who published books on a gospel of grace that presented a radically different view of God and His grace to all I had been taught.

In *What's So Amazing About Grace?* Yancey noted, "The church, says Robert Farrar Capon, 'has spent so much time inculcating in us the fear of making mistakes that she has made us like ill-taught piano students; we play our songs, but we never really hear them because our main concern is not to make music but to avoid some flub that will get us in [trouble].' I have now heard the strains of grace, and I grieve for my friends who have not."[2] That was exactly how I felt.

Grace was new and life changing for me. Living by the rules for behavioral performance made life, in one sense, simple. I was either right or wrong. But freedom can be dangerous, for grace changes everything. I was on a new journey toward that free grace—a journey I've now been on more than forty years. And it is powerfully life giving.

As the early reformer Martin Luther wrote, "I myself have been preaching and cultivating [the gospel of grace] through reading and writing for almost twenty years and still feel the old clinging dirt of wanting to deal so with God that I may contribute something so that He will give me His grace in exchange for my holiness."[3] What truth. What amazing vital grace.

A grace that we all need every day is not a thing; it is found in the giver of it, God Himself.

Grace Leaks Out

No matter how many times we have heard the Good News of God's gracious love freely given to us through Jesus Christ, it leaks out, and we forget and default into trying to find life on our own. We wrongly seek to find our own ways to make life work. Then we hear a song, a sermon, a Bible passage, or experience a tragedy and are "graced again" with the vitality of God's grace. I don't mean we get saved all over again, but we experience what the writer of Hebrews says—that "it is good for our hearts to be strengthened by grace" (Hebrews 13:9), not by working to get it right through our hustle or ambivalence or giving up because of our despair of shame.

In Galatians 2:11-14, we see that the apostle Peter and missionary statesman Barnabas encountered a church filled with non-Jews who were delighted in Christ and the newfound freedom grace had brought their lives. This church was not following the Jewish codes, which bothered them. Peter and Barnabas forgot what grace had done and returned to their moralistic, works-oriented approach to being right and acceptable with God and man. As a result, they practiced racial bigotry toward their brothers and sisters in Christ. When Paul learned of this, he rebuked them to their faces and said that out of fear they were not "acting in line with the truth of the gospel" (v. 14). If God's saving grace can leak out of an apostle who had been with Jesus and a great leader like Barnabas, causing them to live out of their flesh, it can certainly leak out of us. It is one reason the writer of Hebrews warned, "We must pay the most careful attention, therefore, to what we have heard, so that we do not drift away" (2:1).

Pop culture has deeply infected and influenced the North American church in many ways of which we are completely unaware. Engaged Christians are finding that when their children return from the university, they have abandoned the Christian faith and replaced it with another faith.

My friend Gary wept deep sorrowful tears over his daughter Melissa who had come home from her first year at his alma mater. He had been so proud of her being accepted. He wanted to hear how she had learned the chant, and how much she enjoyed the legendary football games and pledging to her sorority. When Sunday approached, Melissa told her parents she didn't want to go with them to church and boldly informed them that she no longer believed in God. She didn't want to fight about it, but she had abandoned the years of their loving, godly guidance. They had prayed and taught her about God, Christ, mission, and loving others. But she believed something different now.

Like Melissa, thousands of others sit under professors who are "missionary evangelists" of the *deconstruction* of Christianity and Western civilization (because it is founded on Judeo-Christian beliefs). It comes as no surprise, since Jesus foretold of the day when we would discover that the world hates us because it hated him first (see John 15:18-19). We have been warned not to love this world's system and to not allow our hearts and minds to be pressed into its mold. Yet thousands are being pressed regularly into the mold of the culture. How do we combat that? How do we keep grace from leaking out? By understanding and practicing *vital grace*.

What Is Vital Grace?

I regularly teach a Gospel Coach training class. When I ask the participants to turn to the person next to them and explain the gospel in one minute, the room explodes in lively activity. At the end of the time, I ask, "How many of you were given a tight definition?" No hands go up. Then I ask, "How many of you heard a story?" All hands go up. This happens because the gospel of grace is Good News and, in its verb form, *gospel* simply means to announce good news. In biblical times, *gospel* was a word used to describe the actions or events (a story of their actions) the Roman emperor had accomplished for the welfare of their world.

The New Testament writers co-opted the word to announce the great action that the true Emperor had accomplished for the world. Hence, the Gospels of Matthew, Mark, Luke, and John tell the story of Jesus—announcing the Good News of who He is and what He has done!

But for us, what does it mean to have *vital* grace? What is the gospel of grace I am referring to? Is it just a Good News story we need to know? Many excellent preachers and writers have addressed the topic. In *God Is the Gospel*, John Piper wrote, "The Christian

Gospel is not merely that Jesus died and rose again; and not merely that these events appease God's wrath, forgive sin and justify sinners; and not merely that this redemption gets us out of hell and into heaven; but that they bring us to the glory of God in the face of Jesus Christ as our supreme, all-satisfying treasure."[4]

Basically, the gospel simply means a story of good news, bad news, and very good news. In the Bible, the gospel of grace is used to refer to the story that God made humans and, in order to address the ruin humans brought to themselves and creation, He sent His Son, Jesus Christ, who, by His life, death, resurrection, and ascension, fully and completely rescued His people and will renew His runaway planet. This story of good news, bad news, and very good news has practical implications for life. The starting point for understanding the vitality of grace for us is God, not us. But something has gone terribly wrong. Life is not the way we sense it is supposed to be.

The 2004 movie *The Village,* written and directed by M. Night Shyamalan, tells the story of a group of families who moved to a protected wildlife reserve after their respective tragedies and escaped from the wicked people in the wicked world. The adults decided to recreate a village of the late nineteen-hundreds and raise their children, who do not know what year it is. The families try to live the simple life, secluded from evil. However, people in the village suffered from fear, physical disabilities, pain, envy, lust, hate, and attempted murder. A love triangle between two men, Noah and Lucius, and a young blind woman, Ivy, ends badly. In a fit of jealous rage, Noah stabs Lucius, trying to kill him. Lucius needs medical assistance, so Ivy leaves the village for help. By her father's instructions she manages to get out of the woods to the "towns." However, toward the end of the movie, we discover that the true year is 2004, and Ivy's grandfather's estate security team guards the preserve.

One point of the movie was that no matter how hard we try to create a "sin-free environment" with "good" people, it will still turn ugly, because we are internally ruined people, and we take our brokenness and pass it along to the next generation. This truth runs counter to our generation's story: namely that we are born basically good people at heart, and society corrupts us. We may be in a cultural moment where a shift is occurring from the traditional view of religion and Christian living in a works/obedience form of rightness to a nonconformist, no-rules-to-follow way of living because "God loves me just the way I am" and that we are already born "right." Does the grace of God still apply to this new world of no rules?

The apostle Paul offered a clear and concise explanation of the message of grace in his first letter to the Christians in the church at Corinth:

> Brothers and sisters, I want to remind you of the gospel I preached to you, which you received and on which you have taken your stand. By this gospel you are saved, if you hold firmly to the word I preached to you. Otherwise, you have believed in vain. For what I received I passed on to you as of *first importance*: that Christ died for our sins according to the Scriptures, that he was buried, that he was raised on the third

day according to the Scriptures (1 Corinthians 15:1-4, emphasis added).

The message of grace is of "first importance." To the believers in the Galatian church, Paul warned that if anyone taught a gospel that was not by grace, let them be under God's curse (see Galatians 1:9). Why? Because the Good News, the gospel, is only good and powerful if it is by grace. Notice, Paul wrote that Christ died for our sins, "according to the Scriptures." Scripture is the authority. What Scripture? He wrote this letter about twenty years after Christ's ascension while pastoring in Ephesus. He had already written to the believers in Galatia ten years earlier, stating, "Scripture foresaw that God would justify . . . by faith, and announced the gospel in advance to Abraham. . . . So those who rely on faith are blessed along with Abraham, the man of faith" (Galatians 3:7-9).

What did Paul mean that Christ died and was raised on the third day "according to the Scriptures"? The Old Testament is what he was referring to. Of course, it begs the question, what did the Old Testament teach about the gospel of grace? We will explore that in greater detail in Chapter Four. But for now, it is clear that the Bible is the authority on the subject of vital grace. The Scriptures speak for God.

Jesus, after His resurrection, told two of His followers walking on the road to Emmaus, "How slow to believe all that the prophets have spoken!" (Luke 4:25). So He went through the Scriptures (the Old Testament) and showed them and explained all that was written concerning Himself. "This is what I told you while I was still with you: Everything must be fulfilled that is written about me in the Law of Moses, the Prophets and the Psalms." Then Jesus "opened their minds so they could understand the Scriptures" (Luke 24:44-45).

I walk my own Emmaus road every day. Like them, I am slow of heart to believe the grace of God. You and I will be hard pressed to cultivate a rich, filled life without knowing the vital nature of grace. But like them, Jesus Himself, through His Spirit, reminds us of His *chesed* (His mercy-love) freely given to us. When grace is center, we will be kept free from becoming a pragmatic moralist or a self-congratulating dogmatist.

How Much Do We Really Need Jesus?

If, like me, you were born and raised in a churched family who sang Christian songs, went to children's church, and/or attended a Christian school, you may not remember a time when you didn't know about Jesus. You were never a "wretched sinner" such as a drunk driver, drug addict, sexual pervert, or murderer. You were never "bad" to the degree that you needed Jesus. In fact, you were taught that you were basically a good kid, but you were a sinner, so if you asked Jesus, He would make up for your sin. You have been taught all your life that you were worth so much that Jesus died for you.

To illustrate, allow me to share a true story from my time as a pastor in a grace-centered church. More than twenty years ago, a national evangelistic team came to the city where I lived and scheduled one night during their evangelistic outreach services as "Youth Night." Our student ministries pastor gathered the teens and parents, and we drove to the event. Of course they offered plenty of singing, "testimonies" from a few celebrities, special music, and one rather intense interview with a man who had been involved in a life of crime, addiction, and prison. He shared a sorrowful story of his childhood and teen years, and how Christ had rescued him from his corrupt lifestyle. It was moving.

On the way home, I listened to the teen girls discussing the service. One girl, who had grown up in an active churched family long before I met her, said, "I sure can see why that guy needed to get saved. His life was horrible." Her thinking, like many others, was that bad people need to be saved by Jesus, but good churched people just need God to help them. Since grace is being given what we do not deserve, it has no meaning or awe to a person who doesn't need to get everything for nothing, because they already have most of what they need. That false belief may be one reason grace is not captivating to this generation.

Unfortunately, thousands of churched and de-churched men and women today who felt guilty or experienced a deep sense of shame growing up and were told to ask God to forgive them, now wrongly think they were "saved" at that moment. They might even have been told to write down the date in their Bible as their second birthday. Many were presented with a Jesus who would forgive the wrong they committed and help them become a better-behaved person. Moral conformity was the aim, and finding relief from a guilty conscience or the crushing feelings of shame was offered by praying a "Jesus prayer."

Some were told that if they asked Jesus to forgive them—perhaps because of lying, cheating on a test, shoplifting candy, fighting with a sibling, breaking curfew, or having a bad mood—they would receive promised forgiveness. In addition, they were told if they asked God to help them not do it again, He would. The bottom line was that they were told they were basically good with a few minor behaviors that could be corrected and their guilty conscience could be assuaged.

Others grew up with a deep sense of shame for what someone did to them or what they did to someone. Shame is a huge issue for the majority world and growing up in a shame-based culture can keep the gospel of grace from penetrating past the scar tissue of the heart.

Fortunately, vital grace covers it all. Consider Werner Mischke's comments in his *The Global Gospel:*

> Imagine if the atonement of Jesus Christ was not only presented as the solution of guilt and condemnation from God, but also as the covering of our shame and the restoration of our honor before God. . . . I submit that communicating the gospel of Christ in such a way that the message includes both the removal of our guilt—*and* the covering of our shame—comprises a more "global" gospel. It is more theologically coherent, reflecting a broader witness of Scripture; plus, it is more congruous to the whole need of deeply depraved humanity—our guilt and shame. Therefore, it is more likely lead to transformation in the Christian life.[5]

Laurel was a talented business administrator at medium-sized firm. Because of her excellent talent and track record, a larger firm hired her. Two weeks into the new job, she had forgotten to file paperwork for a client. It was an oversight. When her boss brought the mistake to her attention, she felt ashamed of herself. *How could I have been so stupid?* and *What an idiot I was* were the thoughts racing through her mind. She felt an inner ugliness. At her church that next Sunday morning, she heard the pastor say, "When we feel shame, a sense of self-loathing, what is being exposed is what we are really living for . . . what we are worshiping as the ultimate value of life." It is okay to feel bad for making a mistake—that is healthy. We just can't dwell on it and allow our mistakes to shame us. The pastor concluded by quoting Dan Allender, "Shame is rooted in our inherent preference to trust false gods rather than depend on God for each and every moment of our existence."[6]

Our current "cancel culture," driven by social media, is based on shame. Most of my upbringing and training in Christianity has been based on a grace focused on God forgiving our guilt for breaking the rules. However, the message of vital grace addresses the issue of shame, not just guilt.

Paul reminded his friends in Ephesus and Colossae that in their natural state they were spiritually dead: "As for you, you were dead in your sins" (Ephesians 2:1; Colossians 2:13). We are not sick, we are dead. Sure, the living dead can do good things (like help neighbors, march for rights, give money to feed the hungry, and clothe the poor), but in their ordinary, everyday lives, there is no spiritual life, and they will eventually die physically as well.

Were you taught you were born dead? Did your parents or Sunday school teachers tell you, "You're dead before God"?

My good friend Tim Barton, Jr. explained once to his boys, "You might hear someone tell you that Jesus came to rescue you from drowning in the ocean, that He dropped you a lifeline to pull you out, but don't you believe it. You were not floating in the ocean in need of rescue. You were facedown dead. In fact, you were dead on the bottom of the ocean floor, and Jesus came in, pulled you out, and breathed into you life-giving breath."

The natural person still realizes they are not the way they were meant to be. Self-righting, whether it takes the path of religion (adhering to religious rules or moral conformity) or the path of nonconformity to religion (following their tribe's rules or making their own), is the only option for this world. The difference between true Christianity and religion is that everything a true Christian does is because he or she is already "right." Both those who are religious and irreligious do everything to try and "right" themselves. This is called *self-rightness*.

Most people own some sense of "rightness" or something they can achieve or become that will allow them and others to find them acceptable. We may use words like *worth, acceptance, favor,* or *welcomed,* which are street words for the big word: *righteousness.* To be righteous really means to be right relationally with someone—yourself or someone else.

You know in your own life that you have tried to "right" yourself in various ways. Think of the last time you had a relational tear, a fight, or a split up with someone. The need for it to be made "right" again was as obvious as the fight itself. How do we make ourselves not just relationally right with others, but make ourselves right again on the inside?

In Gospel Coaching and church vitality ministry, I use a 360-degree evaluation called the Church Leader Inventory™ (for more information, see www.churchleaderinventory.com). I have conducted more than one thousand interviews, reviewing self-evaluations that six observers also evaluate who were invited to share their insights on the leader. We look at the observers' ratings, checking for any gaps between the self-rating and the mean rating of those six. By far, the majority of leaders under-rate themselves compared to their observers. The leaders are frequently harder on themselves in many of the areas than their observers are.

When I have the opportunity to explore the gap, often I hear that they do not see themselves as measuring up to their own standards. Even with the attitude of *God accepts me just the way I am,* they still have a hard time.

On the other hand, some rate themselves much higher than their observers and, like the others, their self-perception is skewed. For both, it is an occasion to ask heart questions that are centered in grace dynamics, whether they are living in grace or in works of their own making or in standards to achieve some level of acceptable spirituality.

Our first parents died when they did not believe God and disobeyed one simple ask, and now "all have sinned and fall short of the glory of God" (Romans 3:23). Does the natural person have no love for God? No, it's more than that. They are actually hostile toward God. Your kids were not born spiritually neutral or "kinda good." Yes, they were born as image bearers of God their Maker (with dignity, beauty, meaning, and value), but in regard to their spiritual relationship with Him, they are dead. What part of dead did we miss?

In that spiritual condition, Paul informs us that the "living dead" wander in darkness (*trespasses* is a word for deviating from or getting out of line with the truth) and ethically live independently, with inordinate desires for self-fulfillment, just like the world shouts at us and the evil one whispers to us, "Live for yourself" (see Ephesians 2:1-3). Not only that, but we are naturally "children of wrath" (see Ephesians 2:3; Colossians 3:6). This is a crisis, is it not? We have told a generation of churched people that Jesus wants to bring relief to their guilty consciences and help them manage their bad behaviors, rebuild their damaged self-esteem, and they think they have eternal life with God.

Instead, what we discover is that God "made us alive with Christ even when we were dead in transgressions—it is by grace you have been saved" (Ephesians 2:5). You had no ability to make yourself alive to God. Here is why it is called *vital grace*. It is all by God and from God.

His Counter-Conditional Love

Grace is of central importance to Christianity and is the key word in the New Testament. God is the "God of all grace" (1 Peter 5:10). He rescued us from the dominating power of our reckless selfishness, not by the things we have done but out of His love and life. God, in His very being, is very "rich in mercy" (Ephesians 2:4).

The Greek word Paul used for *mercy* is from the Hebrew word describing God's covenantal or loyal love (*hesed* or *chesed*). His "mercy-love" means He does not give us, based on our condition, what we deserve (judgment, death, and alienation from God). Rather, because He in His very Personhood is uber-wealthy in mercy-love, He made us alive with Christ, raised us up, and seated us with Him in heavenly realms (all in the perfect tense meaning; it is something that is certain—we can take it to the bank!). The cross of Christ satisfies God's claims and expresses God's affectionate love.

God's love has been described as "reckless love" but should we think of God loving us like some teenager driving irresponsibly through traffic in a reckless way? Is His love like a man who, one day, without much thought, decided to walk into an orphanage, pick one of the children, and proceed to adopt? Is that a picture of how God's loving grace is displayed?

It might have a catchy tune or be an inspiring thought in a great book, but might it be more powerful to understand His love as a love that was eternally planned and perfectly carried out by the Lover? Doesn't an expression of love that is well thought out and planned, with great expense, mean more to us than an expression that was spur of the moment, almost recklessly reactive?

God's love is commonly referred to as unconditional—that is, He loves His own without any conditions performed by them. Yes, and amen! We get everything for nothing. Vital grace and amazing grace!

Singer/songwriter Bob Bennett captured his experience of unconditioned love in his "A Song About Baseball," when he wrote of his experiences as a kid playing little league baseball. No matter how well or bad he played, whether he dropped a ball, struck out with both eyes closed, or made a good play, his father would find him after the game, buy him a soda and snack, and drive him home in style. The chorus captured his memory: "None of it mattered after the game . . . he loved me no matter how I played."[7]

But think deeper. Suppose, just for a moment, the love God has for you is more intense and profound than loving you no matter how you played. What if you look at His love through a lens called *counter-conditional love*? Would that change the music in your heart? It did for me. It changed the idea of the grace of God I had been taught in my early upbringing. David Powlison suggests we call it "contra-conditional love."[8] The idea is that God's love certainly is unconditional, in the sense it is not based on anything good in you. But on another level, God's love is counter to your condition. It is not a blind love, as many see unconditional love. He sees your condition—a spiritually dead person, separated from Him—and counter to that dead condition, He chose to put His love on you and give you a new life (He "plays through you," so you have no fear or dread). What joy to rest in a love that did not begin because of some good in you and will not be taken back because of some outbreak from your former life.

Using my example of the man adopting an orphan: What if he went to the orphanage to intentionally adopt the orphaned child of a couple who had hated him and been a rival enemy in business? What if he knew that the little one had been so neglected during infancy that most likely the child would have physical and learning disabilities his entire life and that the cost of adoption would not simply be the payment then but last for the *rest* of life? Yet the man, out of love and compassion for the little child, willingly went through with financial and legal challenges of the adoption. The man's love wasn't reckless or careless, it was amazing and gracious. Thoughtful and planned actions of love mean more than an impulsive or hasty love.

Paul makes the case that it was out of His love for you that God predestined you to be adopted as His child, through Jesus Christ, out of His sheer good pleasure and will, before the creation of the world—meaning before you did anything good or bad (Ephesians 1:4-5). Why? "To the praise of his glorious grace, which he has freely given us in the One [Jesus Christ] he loves" (Ephesians 1:6).

God was not careless of the consequence of His love for you. He knew exactly what the consequences were of pouring out His love— a life of suffering, judgment, and death as a shamed convict hanging on a cross. Greater than that, Jesus knew it would involve not just His physical death but His spiritual separation and alienation from His Father—hell on earth. He did it for one reason: love. Love for His Father and love for His people; God's glory in all things; the rescue of His people and renewal of all things in the universe: that He would reconcile to Himself all things, on earth or in heaven (see Colossians 1:20).

Allow me to repeat the point again: Grace is God giving you everything you need for nothing. It is getting God's favor through Jesus Christ. We get God, the greatest there is in the universe. Grace is getting everything you need for nothing because it is the gift of God and it is vital because it is indispensable to the continuance of life. Grace isn't reckless but it is relentless.

In *Mere Christianity*, C. S. Lewis wrote:

> If there was any idea that God had set us a sort of exam and that we might get good marks by deserving them, that has to be wiped out. If there was any idea of a sort of bargain—any idea that we could perform our side of the contract and thus put God in our debts so that it was up to Him, in mere justice, to perform His side—that has to be wiped out. . . . Every one who has some

vague belief in God . . . has the idea of an exam or of a bargain in his mind. The first result of real Christianity is to blow that idea to bits.[9]

We have a bigger God than the small god of western Christianity. Don't misunderstand, God isn't small, but the western, post-enlightened, well-educated, over-resourced, hard-working North-American Christian is not "God intoxicated." Rather, many are intoxicated by this world and all her offerings, from every corner of entertainment, prosperity, and/or politics. We live half-heartedly, fooling about with this world's offer of money, sex, and fame when we have been given, by vital grace, the riches of God Himself (see Ephesians 1:18; 2:2-7). We have been raised to life and seated with Him in the heavenly realms in Christ Jesus (see Ephesians 2:6). It is counted as something already ours in order that He can show off the surpassing (hyper) wealth of His grace in the ages to come!

Only vital grace can recast the high and glorious God who invites you back into His presence, experience His power, and be renewed back to His purpose of why He made you. There is good news: we are made in God's image. There is also bad news: we are dead. But there is *very* good news: God, through the grace of Christ's death and resurrection has made us alive by faith, so He can show off His greatness and kindness.

As my wife, Rachel, wisely wrote in her private journal, "Glory is given by God, not manufactured by our own human effort and human success. God delights in calling us to an area where his glory shines through us. And we find our greatest joy, glory, and delight in that unique area of calling. Why is God spreading his glory? Because he loves his kids and wants Christ's kingdom of love and light to restore what was lost by the curse."

We need to be done wasting our lives pursuing non-grace and living as if we were dead (see Ephesians 2:1-2; Colossians 3:1-5; Titus 3:3). That is not a lifestyle of grace. We need to be done living as "performers." If we do not live in vital grace, we tend to think when things go wrong or life gets hard that God is not gracious and we complain, "After all I've done for God—and this is the thanks I get from Him." Why? Because we are viewing life as a mixture of personal performance and God's grace. In his classic *Dynamics of Spiritual Life,* Richard Lovelace observed:

> Christians who are no longer sure that God loves and accepts them in Jesus, apart from their present spiritual achievements, are subconsciously radically insecure persons—much less secure than non-Christians, because they have too much light to rest easily under the constant bulletins they receive from their Christian environment about the holiness of God and the righteousness they are supposed to have. Their insecurity shows itself in pride, a fierce defensive assertion of their own righteousness and defensive criticism of others. They come naturally to hate other cultural styles and other races in order to bolster their own security. . . . They cling desperately to legal, pharisaical righteousness, but envy, jealousy and other branches on the tree of sin grow out of their fundamental insecurity. . . . It is often necessary to convince sinners (and even sinful Christians) of the grace and love of God toward them, before we can get them to look at their problems. Then the vision of grace

and the sense of God's forgiving acceptance may actually cure most of the problems.[10]

We have accepted the ongoing lie that the aim of the Christian life is to be more obediently holy than we were last year. We have been asking, "What am I supposed to do for God?" or "What does God want me to do for Him?" That isn't a call of grace, it is a call back to works. It is missing a vital reality that we are a new creation and what was dead is completely gone because Christ made us alive "so that in him we might become the righteousness of God" (2 Corinthians 5:21). Instead, Jesus is asking, "What do you want Me to do for you?"

One day Jesus made a significant offer: "Come to me, all you who are weary and burdened, and I will give you rest" (Matthew 11:28). Here is what He offered: *You who are trying to earn your own salvation through hard work, instead just come to Me, and I will give you rest.* He added, "Take my yoke upon you and learn from me, for I am gentle and humble in heart, and you will find rest for your souls. For my yoke is easy and my burden is light" (Matthew 11:29-30). You are tired and weary because you are trying to earn what can't be earned. He has done the work, so go to Him and find rest from the hustle.

Rachel and I have friends whose five-year-old girl complained of a backache. After a time, they took her to the doctor who ran tests, only to discover she had leukemia. The doctors told them that there was a 96 percent cure rate for the kind of leukemia she had and, if they followed the course of treatments, she would most likely be healed. But the doctor also said, "She is going to feel a lot worse. She will need to have chemotherapy and radiation therapy. She will have to change her diet and be careful about colds and germs. She'll be in and out of the hospital, and she'll be sick a lot for about three years. In fact, the next three months are going to be very hard. But this is the road to healing."

What would you suppose our friends' response was? Would it surprise you if I told you the father said, "Doctor, I can't believe you think you can control our lives like this. Who do you think you are telling us what our daughter can and can't do? Do you think because you're a doctor you can boss us around? You doctors are all the same—so high and mighty, thinking you have the right to run other people's lives like this!" That, we would agree, would be an irrational response to the doctor's prescription to her well-being.

God has offered free grace. God offers *vital grace* today. You can resist Him. You can tell Him off. You may think He's bossy, intrusive, and demanding, but His grace offers healing.

Christianity is living out the gospel of grace throughout one's life. The same thing that made you and me followers of Jesus is the same thing that keeps us progressing as followers of Jesus—namely, we end our own strategies of gaining acceptance in this life and believe in the acceptance we already have in Him. We live our lives following after the One who "loved [us] and gave himself for [us]" (Galatians 2:20).

The apostle Paul wrote that there is "a righteousness from God that is by faith from first to last, [because] the righteous will live by faith" (Romans 1:17). In fact, we are reminded over and over that "the righteous will *live* by faith" (emphasis added). Vital grace is from first to last and tells me: *I am completely accepted in Christ, so I gratefully follow Him*, and not, *I follow His ways in order to earn His acceptance or favor.* Nothing can make us right except the grace of God.

The more you see it as vital grace, the more it will change you and lead you to life wholeness, or as is popular to say today, "flourishing." When we keep one bit of work or hustle or *God helps those who help themselves* attitude, the more we lessen its power to do its work in and through us. The freer we get it, the better it is.

All sorts of Christians want help in living out the new life God gave them. Many wish it were as simple as daily reciting a prayer from the Old Testament or drawing a prayer circle around what they claim in order to receive and obtain their God-given life. Through my own fifty-plus-year spiritual journey, I have longed for the experience that would get me over the top, receive the full work of the Spirit, finally overcome temptation, manage my sins, and stay deeply in touch with God.

I suspect if you are a follower of Jesus, you have had similar longings at various times. That is a good thing. It means you have been graced by God, through repenting of your old ways of running your own life, believed in Christ as your only rescue, and are being conformed into the likeness of the true Human, the One who loved you and gave Himself for you by the power of His Spirit.

Vital grace is an instant fix—you get everything you did not deserve for nothing—in your relationship with God and who you are as a person. You get Jesus' forgiveness, His full perfection, and Spirit—and it did not cost you anything, for "it is by grace you have been saved, through faith—and this is not from yourselves, it is the gift of God—not by works, so that no one can boast" (Eph 2:8-9).

This is an invitation to journey in vital grace and explore how that shapes life. I have worked to put the concepts in real-life experiences and explanations because the church in North America, the Christians in the church, need to have their "breath taken away" by God and His amazing grace.

We need a daily refresher in the Good News of God's grace because we are wandering away, pursuing our selfish desires daily, forgetting what is ours already. Ponder, as you close this chapter, these three realities and reminders that grace is a free gift to you. I trust they will make you smile and give you joy:

(1) We are completely forgiven, so we have nothing to hide. We have no shame.

(2) We are perfectly righteous in Jesus, so we have nothing to prove. We have no guilt.

(3) We are eternally loved, so we have nothing to fear. We no longer need to be afraid.

That is vital grace.

TWO

Understanding the Backstory of Grace

I had always felt life first as a story: and if there is a story there is a storyteller.

G. K. Chesterton, The *Ethics of Elfland*

My friend Frank Batista is a talented painter who lives in Havana, Cuba. I have one of his paintings hanging in my office. On one occasion I shared with him an idea that would capture the story of God's grace. I crudely sketched out my thoughts on a wrinkled paper and gave it to him. He brought his God-given talent in color, design, beauty, and imagination to create an amazing painting.

Imagine a desolate road with inhospitable, harsh desert-like landscape with barren trees and a few birds off in the distance. In the forefront is the dashboard of a 1957 dented and rust-stained Chevy.

You feel as if you are in the driver's seat behind a large steering wheel looking down that long and rocky road.

As you glance in the rearview mirror, you see the beauty of a lush, tropical beach with sunshine and palm trees. On the horizon, just above the dashboard, is a sunrise barely breaking across the line where the earth and sky collide. Off to the left side of the road is one faded gray, weather-beaten, two-story house with a bright red door, clear, clean, and inviting.

In that dark, yet graphic painting, Frank captured the framework of the story of grace. We are all driving a long, ruined road out of Eden, which is clearly in our rearview memory, with a ruined body and rusted soul, lost in the earthly wilderness. We long for refuge and rest, with a hope of a better future. We need a place, a home or substantial city, where we belong. Along the journey lies a bright red door (see Hosea 2:15 and John 10:9) offering a way home. Singer/songwriter Steven Curtis Chapman, who has taught me much about grace through his music, wrote about this reality, in which he states that Jesus made Himself "the doorway that will lead back to the place where life was new . . . where we belong."[1] On our horizon a new day is coming and all things will be made new (Revelation 21:5). We long for that day—that day that offers us the fulfillment of grace.

Until then we live where we no longer have a compelling, cohesive, and transcendent story of our world, our lives, or destiny that makes sense of life's complexities. Almost as if we don't belong here.

The universe, according to the backstory of our culture, has always existed and it exploded into the beauty of the cosmos and eventually progressed into all living creatures on earth, us included. Pop culture affirms we live in a closed, mechanical, and natural world. The bellow is it's "proven science."

I have heard scores of followers in "science alone" argue that they are not living by faith but follow only the science. No matter how much they try to convince me or themselves, it is still a belief system. Even famed evolutionary biologist and anti-Christian author Richard Dawkins wrote, "I cannot know for certain, but I think God is very improbable, and I live my life on the assumption that he is not there."[2] So much for scientific proof. It is a faith system built on certain presuppositional beliefs.

Much of our secular and mechanical world says there is no grand story to life. We are to content ourselves with the limitations of creating our own versions of ourselves—basically writing our own narrative, which we get to live out—because we are a collection of chemicals that burst into being one cosmic morning. There is no storyteller or story to tell. So what do people do? They spend billions of dollars for stories like *Star Wars*, *Harry Potter*, the *Marvel* series, or *The Hunger Games*.

The oppressive nature of their non-story line has ground down any sense of something bigger than the littleness of naturalism and corrosiveness of pure existentialism (that today is all there is). This belief system has served a crushing blow to the lives of millions of people. The rise of existential naturalism is easily linked, by anyone who is willing to see, to depression, drug addiction, suicide, and a total disregard for life.

If you are the result of a cosmic accident, living as a mechanical machine to be self-absorbed, with a zero-sum ending—there is nothing beyond your grave—then there is little compelling reason to struggle. Does it matter if you achieve your goals? No. More importantly, do you matter? Not really. The West's current story is oppressive not freeing. On the other hand, if it really is a zero-sum game, then we can understand why others choose to "live to die with the most toys," pursuing personal gain above everything.

However, even some in the church have reduced the first chapters of Genesis into debate and a test of Christian orthodoxy. They have lost the majesty and supernatural beauty of God singing the universe into existence and instead argue about ages, gaps, literary forms, or God orchestrating an evolutionary process. They have made a religion out of a few chapters in the Bible.

We need to reorient our lives with the help of the backstory of the gospel so we do not miss the wonder of the great power and overwhelming beauty of God. Do not miss the good news that a personal God, out of sheer grace and the good pleasure of His own will, made all we see and made us for Himself. He loves His creation.

He Created It All

Often, the first line of a story is one of the hardest to write. But not for God. The opening line in the backstory of grace is a brief burst of joy: "In the beginning God created the heavens and the earth" (Genesis 1:1). In the book of Job, probably a story before Genesis was penned, God asked Job, "Where were you when I laid the earth's foundation . . . while the morning stars sang together and all the angels shouted for joy?" (Job 38:4, 7).

Have you ever been in a stadium packed full of eighty thousand cheering fans screaming when their team scores? The roar can be both exhilarating and deafening. At Creation, the stars and angels roared with applause and cheers of great joy. They cried in amazement of such beauty and power! Grace—God's unearned favor—is how the backstory begins. He made everything out of a desire to declare, show, and demonstrate His beauty and glory to others. It is real self-giving love. We did not deserve to be made, much less to know God's overwhelming beauty displayed in His glorious universe.

The Bible, as God's revelation to His creation, proclaims a grand transcendent creation that is here by a supranatural origin. By the prefix *supra*, I mean *that which is beyond what is natural.* God, as He revealed Himself, is not some abstract deistic creator, or "uncaused Cause," nor a single person god, but is God the Father, God the Son, and God the Spirit existing with perfect unity in their complexity.

There is a Personal, all knowing, all powerful, all glorious, all beautiful God who made everything we see, and it is an important reality repeated over and over throughout the gospel story:

Where were you when I laid the earth's foundation? Tell me, if you understand. Who marked off its dimensions? Surely you know! Who stretched a measuring line across it? On what were its footings set, or who laid its cornerstone . . .? Who shut up the sea behind doors when it burst forth from the womb, when I made the clouds its garment and wrapped it in thick darkness, when I fixed limits for it and set its doors and bars in place, when I said, "This far you may come and no farther; here is where your proud waves halt"? (Job 38:4-6, 8-10)

The LORD is the great God, the great King above all gods. In his hand are the depths of the earth, and the mountain peaks belong to him. The sea is his, for he made it, and his hands formed the dry land. (Psalm 95:3-5)

This is what the LORD says—he who created the heavens, he is God; he who fashioned and made the earth, he founded it; he did not create it to be empty, but formed it to be inhabited—he says: "I am the LORD, and there is no other." (Isaiah 45:18)

Ah, Sovereign LORD, you have made the heavens and the earth by your great power and outstretched arm. Nothing is too hard for you." (Jeremiah 32:17)

By him all things were created: things in heaven and on earth, visible and invisible. . . . He is before all things, and in him all things hold together." (Colossians 1:16-17)

Every house is built by someone, but God is the builder of everything." (Hebrews 3:4)

The infinite supranatural God made the natural by and out of His love as a Father. The authors of the Apostles' Creed, one of the earliest Christian creeds, began with, "I believe in God, the Father Almighty, Maker of heaven and earth." Why? Because it was important for Christians to affirm in their hearts and minds regularly that God the Father handmade it all.

God is pleased when we believe He is the Maker of all things: "By faith we understand that the universe was formed at God's command, so that what is seen was not made out of what was visible. . . . Without faith it is impossible to please God, because anyone who comes to him must believe that he exists and that he rewards those who earnestly seek him" (Hebrews 11:3, 6).

How to Make a Man and a Woman

In the first century, when Christianity began to wind its way through various cities, regions, and cultural contexts, the Roman world was filled with polytheism (many gods), mythologies (mythical creatures or idols who controlled the world), superstitions, witchcraft, sorceries, naturalists, and followers of Judaism.

Speaking to the elite class of religious and cultural leaders at one of the great centers of the world, Paul confidently proclaimed, "The God who made the world and everything in it is the Lord of heaven and earth. . . . He himself gives everyone life and breath and everything else. From one man he made all the nations. . . . God did this so that they would seek him and perhaps reach out for him and find him, though he is not far from any one of us" (Acts 17:24-27). He gave them a birth story, a true one, if you will. We are God's "offspring" (v. 29).

One of our family traditions is that on each of our kids' birthdays Rachel and I retell the story of their birth. Each one has a unique story about that day—the things that went on, the rush to the hospital, what the doctors said, the events leading up to the birth, and right after. When our kids were younger, they loved hearing those stories and would say, "Tell me about the time the doctor said to you, 'Get out, Mr. Wood,' or when Mom first saw me, or how our family laughed and cried or when Mom asked, 'Is this really our baby?'" Our youngest always enjoyed us retelling how a large tree fell across the driveway and I barely made it to the hospital in time for her delivery. Every birthday since, we look at their pictures in their baby books.

By telling them their stories, they received a sense of value. Each had their own uniqueness and sense of belonging. They had connection. They had a family relationship to others in this world. They had a mom and dad who loved them, nurtured them, looked forward to their arrival, cried and laughed when they did, and prayed for them. We remembered them.

God wrote down our story so we would rehearse it to one another. The fact that we were handmade by grace (that God gave us everything for nothing) begins with His declaration, "Let us make mankind in our image" (Genesis 1:26). Adam was made, bearing the image of the God who created all things, as the summit of all His greatest achievements in His universe.

Israel's King David was shown the reality of His personal creation, and yours by the way, and like most singer/songwriters do when they are awestruck with some personal, life-changing event, the king wrote a song back to his Maker:

You created my inmost being; you knit me together in my mother's womb. I praise you because I am fearfully and

wonderfully made; your works are wonderful; I know that full
well. My frame was not hidden from you when I was made in
the secret place, when I was woven together in the depths of the
earth. Your eyes saw my unformed body; all the days ordained
for me were written in your book before one of them came to be.
(Psalm 139:13-16)

Amazing grace how sweet the sound that made me who I am.

Later, God miraculously made Eve out of the body of Adam, both
bearing His image. Adam and Eve were made by the God of all
grace. They were made of the natural, created from the dirt from
earth and the bone of Adam's bone (see Genesis 2:23), but they were
also made of the supernatural, the life-giving breath of God (see
Genesis 2:7). As He sang creation into existence, God made them
profoundly different from every other living thing (plants, fish, and
animals) because only man and woman were made in the *imago Dei*
(the image of God).

In this backstory, God repeated the creation of Adam and Eve
twice (see Genesis 1:26-28; 2:7, 21-23), and to make sure we do not
miss the exclamation, He doubled His thought: "In the image of God
he created him; male and female he created them" (1:27). He was
very specific. Man and woman, now the highest of all His creative
wonders, are (we can follow the science on this one) uniquely male
(made with one Y and one X chromosome) and female (made with
two X chromosomes, no exceptions), and are full of beauty (truest
moral beauty, pure, holy), temporal meaning (ruling or managing
over creation and all creatures), dignity (high position in the universe
and personal communication with God), and as spiritual beings

(given a soul, the life breath of God Himself), unlike any other creature He made (see Psalm 8:3-8).

Did you notice Moses, who wrote Genesis, spent one chapter informing his readers how the entire space, time, universe, earth, and animals were created? Next he spent one chapter explaining how man and woman were brought into being. Do you get a feel for what is important in the backstory?

The crowning achievement of His creation is man and woman. Worlds were prepared for them. Man and woman were to have dominion over everything. They had moral responsibility, as part of the creation mandate, to care for the earth, animals, and other image bearers (humans), and to work in the creation God gave them.

Ultimately, they were made to have union with God and find their joy and happiness in life in that union. They were made to enjoy life with God and one another, finding God to be the highest good in all creation. It is the purpose of humanity: loving God with all our hearts, with all our souls, with all our minds. This is not some religious language, rather it demonstrates the desire of God to deeply relate and communicate with you and each of His human community.

The backstory of the gospel, the story of how man and woman got here, is true and real, and God wrote it down so we would rehearse it to one another. It is a fact retold through the Bible. The creation of man and woman was very good! (See Genesis 1:31; Psalm 139:13-16; 1 Corinthians 6:12-20; Ephesians 2:10).

The one aspect in all of His creation narrative that God declared "not good" was that Adam did not have human community. Though other animals existed, he was alone as a human. So "the LORD God said, 'It is not good for the man to be alone. I will make a helper suitable for him'" (Genesis 2:18). Human beings want to connect with other human beings because God is eternally relational. We were made with an instinctive desire to love—first God as our Maker and then one another as bearers of His image.

Theologian Francis Schaeffer wrote:

> The most basic teaching of the Bible is that God exists, and what he is, and the corollary of what man is as made in God's own image. We live in a personal universe, and not in an impersonal one. . . . We are not machines, we are not plants, we are not mere animals, but men [and women] created in the image of God—rational and moral. When we were created, we were created for a purpose. And the purpose of our creation, in which all our subsidiary purposes fit, is to be in a personal relationship to God, in communion with him, in love, by choice, the creature before the Creator.[3]

You may not accept the backstory of the gospel. If so, I suspect you do not most likely because you have been taught to think only one way—that there was a natural beginning to humankind and everything else. You may only know the materialistic, naturalistic, evolutionary story of our beginnings. Understand, your belief in this way is not "proven science," it is a theory that must be accepted by faith. We have no scientific method capable of experimenting an event millions of years ago.

I admit willingly that "by faith we understand that the universe was formed at God's command, so that what is seen was not made out of what was visible" (Hebrews 11:3). One of the reasons the

Bible has always been under assault, criticized, and ridiculed is because of its claim of authority as God-breathed revelation of the original design and purpose of humankind. If you want to be serious about your origin, your birth story, you can find plenty of resources available to read, hear, and study.

The creation of all (heaven, earth, man, and woman) was an act of God's unearned favor. God's kind and free grace alone brought the worlds and our lives into being. That makes it quite meaningful.

The Sin Beneath All External Sins

If you were on a game show and were asked to name five of the most significant events in human history, which ones would you offer in your answer? Would you say the birth of Jesus Christ because it split our sense of history into two times? Perhaps the landing and settlement of the Europeans in the Americas? Maybe World War II and the invasion at Normandy? Or the first space flight? Perhaps you would go back to the invention of electricity or the printing press? Those changed the course of world history dramatically. And of course, you would have to offer the invention of computers.

I doubt, however, the event in Genesis 3 would be on the list of any game show answers, even though it is more fundamental to our history than any other event, other than creation itself. At the beginning of Genesis, God spent one chapter explaining how everything we see got here and one chapter (chapter and half) explaining how we got here, as well as why. Then in Genesis 3, God spent one chapter relating one event in the lives of our first parents

(Adam and Eve). It would seem, based just on the amount of story, this event is critical to us understanding our backstory.

All around the world, through all times in history and among nations, humans have known there is a gap between them, others, and God. We need something that makes sense of that common reality. Questions fill our lives: "Why are things in this world the way they are?"; "Why is there such selfishness and harshness in a world that has been around for millions of years?"; and "Why do we sense that people are not living the way they ought to be?" Our current culture's story line does not make sense of our reality. The philosopher who said, "If there is a God, He must be a moral monster because of all the evil in our world," didn't understand the entire backstory of the gospel.

To grasp the grace message of Christianity it is important to know the backstory of Adam and Eve in the first garden. You will not understand the necessity of grace in your rescue if you miss the ruin in the garden and you will not be inflamed by the glory of a coming renewal if you fail to recognize the wonder and grace of creation. Christianity and its core message of a rescue by grace does not make any sense without believing the opening moments of our history.

Our first parents were placed in the garden of Eden, a place from which they were given the responsibility to be co-managers of all of creation (the earth, the fish, the plants, and the animals). They were promised a full comfortable life of perfect relational bliss, an ongoing and uninterrupted relationship of God's approval, and eternal security as God's vice regents in the universe.

God placed before them in the beautiful garden one tree and that tree stood as a symbol of their dependence and allegiance (their love) to their Father God. God graciously said to them, "You are free to eat from any tree in the garden," enjoying maximum freedom and authority, but from one tree "you must not eat . . . for when you eat from it you will certainly die" (Genesis 2:16-17). The tree ultimately declared that they were responsible to their Father, but it also meant that they were His creatures, not their own creator. The essence of God's message was, "Believe Me, trust Me, and obey Me for all your life and wholeness, for I am good to you. Be the creature and I will be your God, so do not be autonomous. If you choose to live in relationship with Me, all will be well with you. But if you do not, you will die."

This tree of the knowledge of good and evil probably didn't look different from any of the other trees. The major difference was the command of God not to eat from that one. It was the choice they were to make. Why? Because real love is bound up with choice. God made them for a loving relationship with Himself, but He did not program them to love Him. They were free to love or not to love. Which would you consider real love—when your spouse, parent, or child says "I love you" or the computer you programmed to say it tells you? The computer does not love you, no matter how many times it may repeat those words.

God made humankind with freedom to love or not love, but Adam and Eve were tempted by Satan, the Evil One. Satan slyly engaged Eve and deceived her by attacking on two fronts: "Did God really say . . . ?" and then added, "You will not certainly die . . . for God knows that when you eat from it your eyes will be opened, and you will be like God" (Genesis 3:1, 4-5).

On the first front he tempted her with *unbelief.* He asked, "Did God say?" He cunningly whispered a lie to her that has reverberated throughout the universe. The lie that says, *God is trying to deprive you of a good thing—knowledge, being like God—and that isn't really fair, is it? What you need is to be god of your own life to really find your fulfillment.*

He was able to separate in Eve's inner thought life God's heart of love from His command to not eat from one tree and introduced doubting God's goodness and love as a Father.

In a peculiar way, it is not unbelief or nonbelief. It is belief. She was tempted to believe the lie that Satan whispered: "You will not die." I saw a license plate that read, "Only Trust Yourself." That really says all our culture has to offer. Yet God said the only way to please Him is by faith, which means to trust in Him. Since the days in the garden, the questions of the heart of man and woman has been "Is God really good?" and "Does He really love me?" Unbelief in God's love and goodness is the sin beneath all external sins.

Your unbelief is not the absence of belief, rather it's redirected belief. When temptation comes, it comes in the form of unbelief, which is actually a redirected belief to rely on yourself. You can choose what or who you will put your faith in but you cannot choose whether or not you will have faith.

Everyone believes in something. Our temptation is always to find something or someone other than God to give a sense of worthiness, security, or personal well-being.

Think of last time you were tempted: "I know God said that lying to my mom is wrong, but it will be better for me to get my way if I lie, so lying is better." That is the unbelief in God when He says that lying will destroy you and destroy your relationship with your mom. It is also a belief that "you won't die"! Or if you are tempted to cheat on your spouse because you wrongly believe that is the way to find happiness and to really be loved instead of working through the struggle you feel in marriage, well, it really is unbelief in God and His loving warning that infidelity leads to relational, societal, and soulish death (see Proverbs 7:21-23). "Trust me," whispers the Evil One, "you won't die."

When you are tempted to (add your thing here), isn't it really a matter for faith? Is God's grace and love for you, His presence in you, enough? Or is there a better way to find happiness, affluence, fame, and peace? That was the issue for Eve and Adam in the moment and that is the issue for you and me.

In the first garden, Satan tried to void out God's warning about not eating from the tree by suggesting, "You will not die." Today he tries to make void God's promise of believing God's offer of vital grace. Jesus said, "Believe in Me and you will live," and the Evil One whispers, "You will not live. You must take life into your own hands. You must earn your own approval and rely on no one besides yourself." Or in the larger culture, "There is no god to believe in. Just trust yourself, follow your heart, and do your own thing."

The second front of temptation was for *their personal autonomy* (independent and disobedient of His known will) and a *do my own thing* approach to life. It means to be *self-ruled*. We want to own God or be god. Our first parents said inwardly, *I want what I want, not what God wants*. This nature exists in the internal attitude of sin and the internal later flows out into the external actions of sin. They were tempted toward independence from God and so are we.

As author Larry Crabb noted, "The human race got off to a seriously wrong foot when Eve yielded to Satan's lie that more satisfaction was available if she took matters into her own hands. When Adam joined her in looking for life outside God's revealed will, he infected all his descendants with the disease of self-management. Now no one seeks after God in an effort to find life. The most natural thing for us to do is to develop strategies for finding life that reflect our commitment to depending on our own resources."[4] Adam and Eve no longer wanted to be the "imago," they wanted to be "Dei."

At the heart of all our sin is the attitude, *I will not allow anyone to rule my life other than myself.* That attitude exists in both a religious person and a nonreligious person. The defiant claim to be autonomous is a sin beneath the outward sins, begun by the unbelief that God is good. As the apostle James wrote, "Each person is tempted when they are dragged away by *their own evil desire* and enticed. Then after desire has conceived, it gives birth to sin, when it is full-grown, gives birth to death" (James 1:14-15, emphasis added).

Adam and Eve's sin of eating from that tree was against the sum of what God wanted of them and us—namely, to love Him with their whole being. Why? Because He is the best thing in the universe. They were made to bring glory to God by centering their lives around Him. However, they chose to love self over anyone and everything.

Immediately after Adam and Eve's decision, they knew they were morally guilty and became afraid of each other and of God. They were psychologically ruined and felt the shame of their actions. By their wicked decision to seek their selfish way, all the creation they were to manage was ripped apart and ruined.

God had warned, "You will die." And though not an immediate physical death, they did face immediate spiritual death. They knew it and tried to cover up their shame and hide from God (see Genesis 3:7-8).

They were cursed by God, losing His approval. And by His judgment, they were thrust out of the comfort and security of their place in Eden.

A friend who is a long-distance runner told me of a time when, while running, he stepped on a small piece of metal that pierced his shoe. After limping home, his foot swelled, so he put medicine and ice on it and then didn't give it more thought. A couple days went by, and his foot remained swollen and then his ankle swelled. He finally went to the hospital where after examining it, the doctor said, "It's a good thing you came in when you did, because if you had waited any longer, we would have had to amputate your foot."

Just like the little piece of metal jabbed my friend, sin jabbed you at your birth: "Surely I was sinful at birth, sinful from the time my mother conceived me" (Psalm 51:5). And it has infected you completely. Paul articulated our sin issue declaring firmly, "There is no one righteous, not even one . . . there is no one who seeks God. All have turned away . . . there is no one who does good, not even one" (Romans 3:10-12) and "All of sinned and fall short of the glory of God" (3:23). You struggle with sin because you were born a sinner.

This one event in the garden of Eden gives us context and understanding. It explains a great deal in our world—such as why a man can walk into a church's prayer meeting and kill or why two high school teens can shoot their classmates. It offers an explanation as to why your marriage suffers such enormous ups and downs or why your mate committed adultery. It offers a reasonable explanation for why we get so sick in mind and body or why your best friend died after a battle of cancer.

Isn't this a reasonable explanation for why when your little beautiful dear child, born in a wonderful, loving, caring home, with perfect grandparents, all of sudden begins to pitch a selfish little fit? Did you ever teach your son how to tell a lie or push another child down to get their toy? Did you ever have one-on-one time with your teenager to discuss the art of breaking curfew or sneaking around?

It is also a reasonable explanation for why you cannot stop the very things you hate doing and do not do the things you know you should do in order for life to flourish. Each of us constantly surrounds ourselves with our self-justifying, self-exalting, self-excusing, and self-glorifying image of our own making. Adam and Eve started the lifestyle of the "do my own thing."

Here is a key principle: What you believe about your sin will determine what you do with your sin. If you do not think God judges justly, then you will live as you want. It may be what you are wishing for, but it is not the way God loves. Ultimately, your sin has caused a gap between God and you. You can deny it. You can blame someone else or unforeseen circumstances. You can try to drug it, booze it, party it, or work it away. You might even try to pay for it yourself by doing something nice or giving money to charity. But did any of that remove the guilt and shame you live with?

Sin is destroying people's inner lives, as well as their physical health, mental health, relational health, and cultural health. Sin enslaves us, destroying our dignity, beauty, and purpose. It is rotting the imago Dei. Sin is a death-sentencing cancer that must be dealt with because He loves us so deeply. A judgment of hell is a reality because love is a reality. We can try to hide our sin, as Adam and Eve did, but God will reveal it.

The Reality of Judgment

God's love for Adam and Eve and all creation demanded immediate judgment. And that judgment was eternal death, separation from the holy, good, perfect, Father-God of the universe. There is a time coming when God will deal personally, "face to face" (see Deuteronomy 7:10), with those who hate Him and who do not love Him and His will. It is an awful, terrifying thought, no doubt.

Yet, even in the face of that reality, we do not believe its truth deep down. We push back that we are not haters. We take offense with the apostle Paul who wrote that we "have become filled with every kind of wickedness, evil, greed and depravity" and that we are "God-haters" (Romans 1:29-30).

We do not understand how we could be God's enemy (see Romans 5:10). We wrongly believe we are born good and assume we have good motives. Sure, we fail some, lose our tempers, lust a bit, maybe even lie, when necessary. We recognize we are not perfect, but we believe we are basically decent, law-abiding, and kind. We care about the poor, our environment, the disabled, and social justice. And, spiritually, we would rather think that *God loves me just the way I am*.

God says that the payment for our sin is death. He said it in the garden, and He has continually said it, all the way to today. He will say it again tomorrow as well. I don't want to spoil your day, but the chances of you dying is one out of one. Why? Because our first parents sinned, and we are born from them. You will die physically, but also spiritually and eternally from the God who made you unless you accept His vital grace. It should be a grief to us that most people will not find out about God's grace until it's too late.

After saying that God loved the world and sent His Son to give eternal life to those who believe in Him, Jesus summed up our condition succinctly: "Whoever believes in [Jesus] is not condemned, but whoever does not believe stands condemned already because they have not believed in the name of God's one and only Son" (John 3:18).

If you have not heard this story before or if you have heard it and have serious doubts, I hope you will, as John Collins wrote:

> Think of the deepest intuitions you have about your own existence: that your life is real and meaningful, that you want others to treat you right, that there is something wrong at the heart of things, that there is still real beauty in the world, that sometimes people do really admirable things, and sometimes really abominable things . . . and that you hope there is some explanation for life's complexities.[5]

Vital grace can help us "make sense of these intuitions" and explain why we long for a place of perfect peace and our own little piece of heaven here on earth.

The effect vital grace has on our lives is diminished when, in our innermost thoughts, we decide that God is so loving He would never judge anyone. Some of us are afraid of being seen as narrow or bigoted to suggest that God would be so unloving as to condemn or judge anyone for them just for being themselves.

Let me restate the principle: What you believe about your sin will determine what you do with your sin. If you say you have no sin or there is no such thing as sin, then you will most likely continue to sin against yourself, others, and God. If you agree you have sinned and can't stop, then there is need for a rescue.

A Grace-Filled Promise

Since the story of grace is a story of rescue, at the moment of failure in the garden, God made an outstanding promise: "I will send a someone to deal with the ruin you made. Do not look inside yourself for rescue or to your own ability to make it right again." It was God's shout of vital (very necessary) grace in the midst of the judgment. He spoke to the Evil One who led the rebellion, "I will put enmity [root word of *enemy*, meaning hatred and hostility] between you and the woman, and between your offspring and hers" and promised that the coming One "will crush your head, and you will strike his heel" (Genesis 3:15). He promised a Rescuer who will be "pierced" (killed for our sin; see Isaiah 53:5), but nevertheless, will be the victor over evil and death with a crushing defeat.

Is there a more sobering and terrifying expression of God's eternal hatred for sin and His just response for those who are enemies than what we find in the Cross? When His beautiful, loving, wondrous, and life-giving Son, Jesus Christ, cried out in deep lament, "Why have you forsaken me?" (Matthew 27:46), we discover a deep sense of grace. A most perfect idea of grace. We, through Him being punished in judgment for our sins at His death, get something for which we did nothing. However, it wasn't nothing to God, as He paid the price for our heinousness and gave to us all His goodness to make us His friends. Since you can't be "gooder" (more right) than Jesus, grace is essential to getting life of friendship with God.

Passing It On

The problem Adam and Eve created, as we have seen, was passed down to the next generation. In Genesis 4 we discover their firstborn son, Cain, whom they thought was the "man" to come and rescue (Eve said after his birth, as recorded in verse 1, "With the help of the LORD I have brought forth a man"), was actually a murderer. He killed his brother, Abel, in a jealous rage. The backstory quickly moves along as the writer sped through time, like pressing fast forward on the television remote, from Adam to Noah. When the writer pressed "Play" again, we discover that the world was now filled with "Cains." Every person was living for him/herself as their own god and in independent defiance of the One who made them. God said, "Enough" and judged the world with a flood.

In order that He might redeem for Himself a people (see Titus 2:14), He selected by grace one man Noah, who by faith in God as the true Rescuer, along with his family, found their rescue in a large watercraft called an ark. After the earth's destruction, the backstory moves quickly through time and we find ourselves in a world filled with people, once again, bent on finding their own way by erecting a stairway to heaven and wanting to "make a name for ourselves" (Genesis 11:4). God disrupted their rebellious plans and separated the nations and scattered the people by language and geography.

We may tend to think of ourselves as basically nice and well-intentioned, who may have a few bad habits, but, in reality, we are still God doubters and disobedient children. Paul explained it this way: "Just as sin entered the world through one man [Adam], and death through sin, and in this way, death came to all people, because all sinned . . . death reigned from the time of Adam . . . judgment followed one sin and brought condemnation. . . . Consequently . . . through the disobedience of the one man the many were made sinners" (Romans 5:12, 14, 16, 18-19).

C. S. Lewis observed: What Satan put into the heads of our remote ancestors was the idea that they could "be like gods"—could set up on their own as if they had created themselves—be their own masters—invent some sort of happiness for themselves outside God, apart from God. And out of that hopeless attempt has come nearly all that we call human history—money, poverty, ambition, war, prostitution, classes, empires, slavery—the long terrible story of man trying to find something other than God which will make him happy.[6]

At first blush, some people recoil at the idea that because one person rebelled against the Creator God and wanted to be his own god everyone else is held responsible. How can it be fair that one person's decision impact my life? But if you consider your own story, everyone before you in your ancestry made choices that impacted you. Every single one of them.

One of the television shows my wife enjoys is *Finding Your Roots*. In one episode, actress Queen Latifah was the guest. As the host Henry Louis Gates, Jr. revealed her family's history, he asked her to turn the page of the book in front of her and read what was there. The document said, in part, "Being conscientious of the injustice and impropriety of holding my fellow creature in state of slavery, I do hereby emancipate and set free one Negro woman named Jug, who is about twenty-eight years old, to be immediate free after this day, October 1, 1792, Mary Old."

Gates said, "You are looking at the moment that your family became free."

Queen Latifah responded, "What must that have been like, to know this, to know you are free. What must she have been thinking?"

Gates said, "On September 30, 1792, she was a slave. The next day, she was free, all because of this woman. She decided it was morally wrong."

Queen Latifah smiled. "People still think that one person can't make a difference. One person made a difference to my whole entire family line. Mary Old, one person, made a difference."[7]

Indeed, one person's choice in the past changed the direction of my life, too. In the early 1920s, my grandfather decided to emigrate from England with his wife and their son (my father) and move to the United States. I had nothing to do with the decision, but because he made the choice to leave Newcastle Upon Tyne, England, for Boston, Massachusetts, I exist as an American. His one decision affected my whole existence and now the existence of my children and their children. Finding your roots goes all the way back to Adam and the decision he made affected you. You were made in God's image but born with a death curse.

We Are Ready for Rescue and Renewal

What does our backstory have to do with vital grace? From Genesis 12 (the call of Abraham) to the present, God is on a mission to rescue His lost children from the disaster that occurred in the garden. We lost everything. We have nothing. We are under a curse. We tried to work it out on our own, building a life for ourselves, but we discovered we need everything because we have nothing.

The writer of Proverbs reminds us that "there is a way that appears to be right"—it seems like the way to go—but it leads away from life (14:12). Have you learned this truth yet? We set out with a plan for how to make things work out well and somewhere along the road we realize we are in way over our heads and we feel like we are drowning. The wise writer of the Proverb was right: it seemed right at the time but in the end it leads to death.

Our doubting God and relying on ourselves has only brought us to enslavement and social fracture: basically nowhere. Wouldn't it be freeing to discover that there is a way to have Someone give us everything we need, not because of what we can produce, but by His free grace?

The answer to your problem with sin is not a "what" but a "Who." God did send a Man, "born of a woman" (Galatians 4:4), who became the curse for us (Galatians 3:13). And that Man, Christ Jesus, is the only mediator between God and humanity (1 Timothy 2:5). The gospel story is about God rescuing His lost children by His grace alone through Christ's life, death, resurrection, and ascension to the throne as King. He is renewing and He will renew what was ruined because of that grace. The backstory gives us the "why" we need rescue, grace, and renewal.

The entire gospel story, moving forward from Genesis 12 to Revelation 21, explains how God is on a mission to rescue His children and renew His runaway planet. He will do everything that we cannot do. He came Himself and began a new kingdom. As Revelation 21 promises: One day the King of all creation, the King of love, will return. And when the first earth passes away, the New Jerusalem will come down from God. It will not need the sun or moon because the glory of God will give it light. God Himself will be on the new earth. All the nations will live in the light of His glory. Those who have received His grace will be His people and He will be their God.

THREE

Our Vital Rescue

*The promise comes by faith, so that it may be by grace
and may be guaranteed to all Abraham's offspring—
not only to those who are of the law but also to those
who have the faith of Abraham. He is the father of us all.*

Romans 4:16

Reading the backstory of the story of grace may leave us asking, "Is rescue possible?" or "Can this runaway world be renewed?" The first eleven chapters of Genesis alone can make us wonder, *Is there any hope for the human condition since we are left under a curse?*

To answer the need of our rescue and world renewal, we might think, as with most stories, that the opening scene would introduce us to a young child who would eventually become the hero. Perhaps we would meet a youthful warrior in training like Luke Skywalker or Rey in *Star Wars*, or a William Wallace in *Braveheart*, or a strong princess such as Fa Mulan, or Elena Ransom in *The Firebird Unit*, or even an unassuming boy like Harry Potter, who was trained to be *the one* for a certain moment.

And that is how we were set up in the backstory of Creation. We needed someone to come for us and do for us what we are unable to do for ourselves. From the moment our first parents chose to try to be gods themselves, their decision has reverberated down throughout the long and sad history of humankind away from God.

Yet the story of grace begins the global rescue of the planet with a seventy-five-year-old childless man and his wife from the desert plains of what is present-day Iraq. God regularly chooses to start with things that are seemly impossible. When God does this, He commonly uses weak things, foolish things, splendid sinners, people who lack influence, miserable misfits who lack financial resource or physical strength, and/or people whom the world considers nothing, so no one can mistake who is actually rescuing and renewing. God's kind and free grace is the grand and only resource for us all.

The rescue story by grace alone begins with Abraham, who remains a major figure in the ongoing story. From Genesis 12 on, God's promises are fulfilled by Abraham's relationship with God. And we find a core doctrine in Christianity that is grounded in a statement about Abraham: "Abraham believed God, and it was credited to him as righteousness" (Genesis 15:6; Romans 4:3, 9, 22).

Author and theologian Christopher Wright observes, "The call of Abraham is the beginning of God's answer to the evil of human hearts, the strife of nations, and the groaning of brokenness of his whole creation. It is the beginning of the mission of God and the mission of God's people."[1] If you want to understand your own grace story and vital rescue, you will need to know Abraham's story because our stories flow from his.

Who Is This Abraham?

Abram, his name before God's intrusion into his life, was from a city called Ur. The city was sophisticated for its time and perhaps the largest city in the known world, with some sixty-five thousand people or 0.1 percent of the world's population.[2] It was a commercial center, since it had a seaport that allowed for lots of trading. The area had a considerable number of farms and ranches, and Abram might have owned one of them. Ur was also known for its higher education, teaching mathematics and languages. Being cosmopolitan, it enjoyed a reputation for its polytheism. A large temple structure, Ziggurat of Ur, had been built (probably one like the first tower at Babel) that allowed its citizens to worship several different deities.

Abram and his family, like all their neighbors, were idol worshipers, probably following the moon god, Lunar (see Joshua 24:2). Abe is not the typical hero. He wasn't looking for God or to rescue anyone, but his story is foundational to understanding the whole rescue story of grace because, from this point forward, God refers to Himself as "the God of Abraham" (e.g. Genesis 26:24; Exodus 3:6; Psalm 105:8; Matthew 22:32). He doesn't ever make promises or vows because He is the "God of Noah" or the "God of Adam," but because "I am the God of Abraham." Abraham stands alone as the Father of all who believe the gospel of Christ (see Romans 4:11). Interestingly, three of the world's most influential religions—Judaism, Islam, and Christianity—all look to Abraham as their father.

And yet Abram had no children. He was a wealthy businessman who, at the age of seventy-five, rightly assumed, along with his wife, Sarai, that they would not have anyone with whom to share their fortune. They bore the cultural shame of barrenness. But God broke through the darkness and by shear grace loved this man, revealing Himself to him.

We can best understand Abraham's journey in a few key chapters in Genesis. The development of his story is God's answer to the problem of our rebellion to God's love and authority. God began with one lost old man and loved him. Why did God decide to love the idol-worshiping Abram? Because He loved him. That sounds circular, I know, but listen to the words of Moses explaining the call of God to the Israelites: "The LORD did not set his affection on you and choose you because you were more numerous than other peoples, for you were the fewest of all peoples. But it was because the LORD loved you and kept the oath he swore to your ancestors [Abraham, Isaac, and Jacob]" (Deuteronomy 7:7-8).

Several chapters later, he adds: "The LORD set his affection on your ancestors and loved them" (Deuteronomy 10:15). Why did God choose Abram? Because He loved him. According to apostle Paul, God preached the gospel to Abraham: "Scripture foresaw that God would justify the Gentiles by faith, and announced the gospel in advance to Abraham" (Galatians 3:8).

Though Abraham's grace story is long, we can focus on four vignettes that mark the progression of the gospel being revealed to him: *Grace for Nations, Free Grace, Grace for Each Generation,* and *Grace from the True Son.* Abraham, no doubt, did not understand everything we know (being able to look back at the meaning now that Jesus has come), but he did have the gospel given to him and he did believe God.

Vignette #1: Grace for the Nations

To begin reaching the nations of our runaway planet, God called Abraham to get out of his homeland and go to a place the Lord would show him. The call to go is literally "going-go" to the land of promise. It is not a land that Abraham would work for, but a land he would receive as God's gracious gift to him:

> The LORD had said to Abram, "Leave your country, your people and your father's household and go to the land I will show you. I will make you into a great nation and I will bless you; I will make your name great, and you will be a blessing. I will bless those who bless you, and whoever curses you I will curse; and all peoples on earth will be blessed through you."
> (Genesis 12:1-7)

At the close of the backstory (Genesis 11), we learned how the people had been scattered across the globe and multiple nations established. God is a God whose aim is to reach all the nations with His gospel of grace. God's gracious promise was to justify the Gentiles (the nations) by faith, and He gave the promise, "I will bless you Abraham to be a blessing to the nations" (Genesis 12:2-3).

Christopher Wright notes, "Now the main point of God's promise to Abram was not merely that he would have a son, and thereby descendants who would be especially blessed by God, but that through that people of Abram God would bring blessing to all nations of the earth. . . . There is a universal scope and perspective to him and them: one nation for the sake of all nations."[3]

It is foundational to the whole story of grace that we see from the outset that God has very good news for the nations or peoples of the world. Vital grace is not for one people group, race, or culture. It is not an American thing. It is fundamentally a gospel of grace for *all* the earth! No one has to earn their way back to God. Anyone can get something for nothing, not just you and me.

We need to recover the full scope of God's vital grace that says God is doing something about the condition of the world. It turns us away from a self-preoccupation of what God is only doing for "me" to what God is doing in the world.

The God of all grace is cosmic in His scope. He came to reverse, through a gospel of grace to the nations, the effects of the worldwide curse our first parents Adam and Eve originated. That way no one can boast that "I worked my way back to God."

Jesus Himself reminded His disciples of the international scope of His grace when He told them to "go into all the world with God's grace, starting in your Jerusalem, moving into your region and to the nations" (Matthew 28, my paraphrase). He is on a mission. He has a people for His mission. And you are to be on His mission. One day multitudes from "every nation, tribe, people and language" will worship Christ together (Revelation 7:9) because Abe, in faith, began a worldwide movement of grace.

Vignette #2: Free Grace

Abraham had been promised a son, an heir, but he and Sarah were in their nineties by this time and still without children. Years had gone by since God had said He would give him a son. And finally God spoke:

> The word of the LORD came to Abram in a vision: "Do not be afraid, Abram. I am your shield, your very great reward." But Abram said, "Sovereign LORD, what can you give me since I remain childless? . . . You have given me no children. . . . Then the word of the LORD came to him: . . . "a son who is your own flesh and blood will be your heir." He took him outside and said, "Look up at the sky and count the stars—if indeed you can count them." Then he said to him, "So shall your offspring be." Abram believed the LORD, and he credited it to him as righteousness. (Genesis 15:1-7)

Abe basically asked God, "Where's the son—the man—You promised us? What will You give me to show me that Your promise is true?" And God said, "Look at stars, count them. That is how many children you will have."

The late singer and songwriter Rich Mullins wrote a song "Sometimes by Step" that captured Abe's encounter with God and remembered "how one star he saw had been lit for me," because thousands of years later, God's grace was given to Rich.[4] We can say the same: that one of those stars represented you and one represented me.

The story continued as Abe responded to the promise with reasonable curiosity:

> Abram said, "Sovereign LORD, how can I know that I will gain possession of it?" So the LORD said to him, "Bring me a heifer, a goat and a ram, each three years old, along with a dove and a young pigeon." Abram brought all these to him, cut them in two and arranged the halves opposite each other; the birds, however, he did not cut in half. Then birds of prey came down on the carcasses, but Abram drove them away. As the sun was setting, Abram fell into a deep sleep, and a thick and dreadful darkness came over him. . . . When the sun had set and darkness had fallen, a smoking firepot with a blazing torch appeared and passed between the pieces. On that day the LORD made a covenant with Abram and said, "To your descendants I give this land." (Genesis 15:8-12, 17-18)

Abraham asked again, "How will I know this is true?" He was not doubting, but in faith asking God to provide him with some answer. God told Abraham to collect particular animals (these will be used later in Israel's sacrificial system), cut them in half, and lay them out on the ground. He then fell into a deep sleep and had a vision. A smoking firepot and blazing torch passed between the pieces. God, who shows up as a pillar of fire and cloud of smoke later, is demonstrating His grace—Abe will get something for nothing. God will have to pay the price, but to Abe it was free, unearned grace.

We don't understand what is being done because we only write up contracts or memorandums of understanding, sign, and seal them. If you buy a mortgage for land or a house, you sign a paper promising to pay the owner or lender a certain amount of money. It's true with every contractual agreement you make today, from leasing a car to owning a cell phone, you have to provide a signature (digitally or in ink).

They had a different culture. Abraham understood what was going on because this concept was common to him. He might have done this in his own business ventures once or twice in Ur. In those days, when someone was going to sell or give a person land or enter into any formal contract, the person made a promise, cut up an animal, and both parties walked through it. The person made a promise and if he didn't keep the terms (he was the goat), the same thing that happened to the animal would happen to him.

What Abe never imagined was that God alone made the walk. It was truly amazing. God was saying, *I make this with you. I will keep both parts of the deal, because I am giving you everything for nothing.* "The truly amazing thing about the whole incident," writes author Steve Brown, "is that it was God—and God alone—who walked down the path between the cut-up animals. God was saying that Abram wasn't required to do anything."[5] God kept both sides of the deal.

Abraham faltered, of course, and relied on his human ingenuity to try and help God out. He relied on himself and used his wife's servant woman, Hagar, to give him a son. She gave birth to Ishmael, son of his flesh not faith, and he became the father of the Persians.

Ultimately though, Abraham believed God:

> The promise comes by faith, so that it may be by grace and may be guaranteed to all of Abraham's offspring [that's you, if you are a follower]. . . . He is the father of us all. As it is written, "I have made you a father of many nations." He is our father in the sight of God, in whom he believed—the God who gives life to the dead and calls into being things that are not were not. . . . he did not waver through unbelief. (Romans 4:16-17, 20)

Abe believed in the promise of an heir, but he wasn't simply looking for a son so he could hand out cigars to his buddies or so he'd have a namesake. He was looking for the promised man of Genesis 3:15—a man who was to come who would crush Satan's head and take care of the mess. Abe believed the grace story that God will provide the Man of the Promise.

Part of the mystery of grace is that God is able to take one event in the life of a character and demonstrate His grace through it. The clear gospel of grace in this historical event is that God did come one day and keep the deal.

Even though Jesus did not fail His part, still He was "cut to death" because we did not keep our part of the deal. By our choice to alienate ourselves from God the Father, He made God the Son (also called the Son of Man), who didn't have any ruin or rebellion, to be ruined for us, so that we might have the promised renewal. As Paul wrote, "The words 'it was credited to him' were written not for him alone, but also for us, to whom God will credit righteousness—for us who believe in him who raised Jesus our Lord from the dead. He was delivered over to death for our sins and was raised to life for our justification" (Romans 4:23-25).

Abraham got something for nothing. He received something he did not deserve, and we do as well. That is great news!

Vignette #3: Grace for Each Generation

One of the confusing things for people who are not "churched" is how many different types of churches and Christian beliefs there are. There are a lot of different brands and it bothers and confounds them. Skeptical people who don't understand why there are differences simply see it as one more reason for them not to believe. They reason that if Christianity were true, then everyone would agree on everything.

Yet one reason for the differences has to do not with the larger story of God's grace to us, but with some particulars of the story. I value the differences. We are not a bland group of pale, cookie-cut, and photocopied followers.

One issue Christians have debated, for instance, is whether one believes God works down family lines or works only individually. Those who see God working down family lines look back to an understanding of the story of Abraham. In Genesis 17, God told Abraham, "As for me, this is my covenant with you: You will be the father of many nations. No longer will you be called Abram; your name will be Abraham, for I have made you a father of many nations. I will make you very fruitful; I will make nations of you, and kings will come from you" (vv. 4-6).

But then, God enlarged Abe's understanding of the relationship the grace He had given him and his family:

I will establish my covenant as an everlasting covenant between me and you and your descendants after you for the generations to come, to be your God and the God of your descendants after you. . . . As for you, you must keep my covenant, you and your descendants after you for the generations to come. This is my covenant with you and your descendants after you, the covenant you are to keep: Every male among you shall be circumcised. You are to undergo circumcision, and it will be the sign of the covenant between me and you. For the generations to come every male among you . . . those born in your household or . . . those who are not your offspring. . . . [It] is to be an everlasting covenant. (Genesis 17:7, 9-13)

In the development of God's grace, God gave Abe a way to outwardly express the inward heart change that had happened to him personally. Circumcision, the physical cutting away of flesh, was given to Abraham, and then to his sons to signify His work done for them. The sign indicated the need for cleansing and the process of that cleansing, the cutting away, in a judgment of sorts (bloody) and the healing newness from that judgment. And notice it was given to two people groups: those born into his household and those not of his offspring.

Abraham was to circumcise *every* son born into the "family" and to *all* adult males brought into the family. It was a forever covenant. As Abraham's children, we are included in the family.

In the backstory we learn that Adam and Eve's personal ruin and alienation had been passed along to their sons, Cain and Abel (see Genesis 4). That the ruin continued to be passed down is self-evident, yet God's grace is to move down family lines and to work through grandparents, parents, and their children, and through as many generations who remain faithful to His promise.

When Christ came, the fulfilment of the outward expression was now found in His bloody death, and He took all the punishment and judgment of God. As Peter, Christ's apostle, announced to the new believers in Acts 2:39: "God's promise is for you and for your children." So in the early stories of God's grace saving lives, one important clue to the inclusion of families is that entire households were said to have believed and been baptized (see Cornelius, Acts 10; Lydia's household, Acts 16; the jailer's household, Acts 16; Crispus's household, Acts 18; and Stephanas's household, 1 Corinthians 1). God still works down family lines. We receive all the blessings that Abraham received and more.

Many churches use different forms to celebrate or acknowledge God's desire to work down through families. Some have child dedication, while others use baptism. Though baby dedication, christening, and infant baptism are not the same thing, they express the desire to see God's love and grace be passed down into the lives of the children of Christ followers.

Paul wrote to clarify what God was doing by working His love and grace down from one generation to the next when wrote:

[Abraham] is then also the father of the circumcised who not only are circumcised but who also follow in the footsteps of the faith that our father Abraham had before he was circumcised. It was not through law that Abraham and his offspring received the promise that he would be heir of the world, but through the righteousness that comes by faith. . . . Therefore, the promise comes by faith, so that it may be by grace and may be guaranteed to all Abraham's offspring—not only to those who are of the law [Jewish descent] but also to those who have the faith of Abraham. He is the father of us all. (Romans 4:12-13, 16)

We are now adopted sons and daughters of God. As Christian theologian James Packer wrote, "Our first point about adoption is that it is the highest privilege that the Gospel offers: higher even than justification . . . In adoption, God takes us into His family and fellowship and establishes us as children and heirs. Closeness, affection and generosity are at the heart of the relationship. To be right with God the judge is a great thing, but to be loved and cared for by God the father is a greater thing."[6]

If you are a parent, God is working from you down into your children's lives. You are to pray with and for each child. You have a unique opportunity to demonstrate grace to them. Both their need and your need for grace. Through you, they begin to form an idea of what God is like. You could raise them to be focused on good moral behavior or on becoming well-educated and financially secure. However, neither will save them from their own spiritual ruin. You get a choice in what you will do in their stories to lead them to see the all-sufficient grace God has offered to them for life.

If you are single, you have a grand opportunity to become a spiritual parent to others. God still wants to work down into the lives of others through you. Perhaps it is with others in church or at a local shelter, or being a mentor. Maybe God is calling you to engage in foster care, adoption, or child sponsorship with a Christian agency. Grace can be demonstrated and shared through the lives of singles or childless couples.

Through our Father of faith, God has promised a new community based on His overwhelming love; a renewed mission for us; a kind hope for our families; and a restored vision for our future.

Vignette #4: Grace from the True Son

Now in the story we find one last gospel vignette. Abe and Sarah were one hundred and ninety years of age respectively when they miraculously had a son named Isaac, which means laughter. Life seemed great, God had provided an heir of their estate. And then one day God showed up again. This time to test Abraham's faith. God told him to take "his only son" Isaac and sacrifice him on Mount Moriah.

Once again, we find language that would be familiar to Abraham in the command to take Isaac and "going-go" to the place God would show him. He couldn't have missed the promise from the first day he heard God say "[going-go] to the land I will show you."

If you are unfamiliar with the story, I suspect that questions come: *Why would God command Abe to murder his son? Did Abraham commit some horrible sin that warranted his sacrificing his son? Isn't this a violation of God's own law against child sacrifice? Isn't this a form of cosmic child abuse?* These are questions the deconstructionists raise in challenging the grace of the gospel.

In *Counterfeit Gods*, Tim Keller explains this story in a compelling way:

> If Abraham had heard a voice sounding like God's saying, "Get up and kill Sarah," Abraham would probably never have done it. He would have rightly assumed he was hallucinating, for God would not ask him to do something that clearly contradicted everything he had ever said about justice and righteousness. But when God stated that his only son's life was forfeit, that was not an irrational, contradictory statement to him. Notice, God was not asking him to walk over to Isaac's tent and just murder him. He asked him to make him a burnt offering. He was calling in Abraham's debt. His son was going to die for the sins of the family. Abraham was faced with the ultimate question: God is holy. Our sin means that Isaac's life is forfeit. Yet God is also a God of grace. He has said he wants to bless the world through Isaac. How can God be both holy and just and still graciously fulfill his promise of salvation?[7]

The writer to Hebrews informs us that, by faith, when God tested Abraham, Abe offered Isaac as a sacrifice, even though God had said to him that Isaac was the son who was promised to him, because he reasoned that God could raise the dead and figuratively speaking he did receive Isaac back from death (read Hebrews 11:17-19). Isaac went willingly, not as a victim of abuse.

His "death and resurrection" pictured the True Lamb and True Son who was to be killed. Romans 4, verses 11 and 17 remind us that he believed in God, who gives life to the dead and calls things that are not as though they were! Abe, Jesus said, desired to see Christ, so to "see Him," he had to hike up Mount Moriah with Isaac and sacrifice him, then Abe got to "see" Christ. Abraham called the place *Jehovah-Jireh*, meaning the "Lord provider" because the Lord did provide: He provided Himself! Abraham "saw" his coming death and resurrection and was glad (see John 8:56).

We learn just how great the love of the Father is toward us that we could be called children of God. Astonishing. It is the "wow" of vital grace and it should take our breath away: "This is how God showed his love among us: He sent his one and only Son into the world that we might live through him. This is love: not that we loved God, but that he loved us and sent his Son as an atoning sacrifice for our sins" (1 John 4:9-10). The Father led His one and only Son up a hill to a cross to lay on the altar willingly, so to speak. Keller added, "Jesus alone makes sense of this story. The only way that God can be both 'just' (demanding payment of our debt of sin) and 'justifier' (providing salvation and grace) is because years later another Father went up another 'mount' . . . with his firstborn and offered him there for us all."[8]

If we see this event only as an example for us to follow, that we must do as Abe did and lay down our Isaacs (our idols, heroes), and not as an act of grace, then we might end up believing that we could somehow merit our way to God by being more committed.

But what if this event isn't about you and what you sacrifice for God but what He has already done for you? Oh, we do learn that God requires total sacrifice, but the stunner is that He provided the sacrifice Himself. Isaac wasn't enough. And neither are your "Isaacs." It really is by grace alone.

God's words to Abraham, "Now I know you love me because you have not withheld from me your only son" reminds us of another Father: "He who did not spare his own Son, but gave him up for us all—how will he not also, along with him, graciously give us all things?" (Romans 8:32). The cost of your new life is everything. And since God provided it Himself and has given it to you freely, Abe's example is to receive what God has done for you by faith. The hymn writer Charles Wesley summed it up well: "Amazing love how can it be that Thou my God should die for me?"[9] It was a rescue mission and it was accomplished. Abraham and the promise are pointing us to Christ. The Bible does not say "and to seeds," meaning all Abe's descendants, but "to Seed," meaning one person, who is Christ (Galatians 3:16).

What story do you want your life to tell? Every day you are making decisions that turn your life one way or another. Though you have little to no control over life's circumstances, you're in good company because neither did Abe. But one reality remained core to his story: the grace of God freely given to him changed his entire worldview and the trajectory of his life.

Relentless Grace

How many years was God engaging His relationship with Abe and Sarah? He went on a twenty-five-plus year journey of relentlessly pursuing them with His grace. Sure Abe failed, redirected his belief, tried to manipulate the situation, help God out, and try to do His part. He often relied on himself, but grace kept coming at him. Abe was reckless with the treasure God had given him, but God was not deterred, instead He kept in loving pursuit of Abraham. That is the relentless grace of God.

The God of all grace was relentless in His dialogue with Abe. He spoke to him. Abe spoke back. Prayer, our ongoing dialogue/communication with God, is far from me telling God how to run my life or giving Him advice on how He ought to run His universe. Rather, it is the conversation of the pursuing God with His loved ones. Abe learned to love others more than himself because of the grace he had been given by God (for instance, Genesis 18:20-33 describes how he pled with God for Sodom not to be judged).

Yes, Abe believed God's promises. I think Abe repented for his self-reliance. He obeyed by faith when he left his homeland. He looked ahead to a new city. He sacrificed. He also had an active-passivity in his life. But it was all and only because of God's relentless pursuit of his heart and life. God wanted him to know real life—the vitality of life in knowing God, even Jesus Christ (John 8:56 says that Abraham rejoiced when He saw Jesus and was glad). It is what we were made for. Abe loved God because God first loved him, and we love God because He first loved us.

One of the outcomes of God's unrelenting grace was that Abe became the first disciple-maker. He is the "father of all of us who believe." Abraham disciples us to grow in "the faith" (in God who "gives life to the dead and calls things that are not as though they are"), not in our faith. He showed the way grace operates.

God's relentless grace for Abe and you and me was demonstrated in the willing sacrifice of the True Son, the True Seed, the True Man, who "rescued us from the dominion of darkness . . . in whom we have redemption, the forgiveness of sins" (Colossians 1:13).

Beware of the Dogs

Someone sent me a picture of two dogs lying in the grass, their feet up, appearing to be laughing and having a good time. One dog is saying to the other, "Then he said, 'Come in. Don't worry, he doesn't bite.' And I bit him." When I see a *Beware of the Dog* sign, I don't have to be warned twice. Having been bitten once, "beware" and "stay away" make sense to me.

Paul hung up a "BEWARE OF THE DOG" sign when he warned his Christian family in the church at Philippi because false teachers were making false claims. They were teaching that Jesus wasn't enough to earn God's favor and that it didn't matter what they did in their bodies because the body was worldly not spiritual, so they could live any way they chose. We have some of that around today. Neither of those teachings are the gospel of grace.

We too must beware of any teacher, no matter how bright, articulate, or educated, who claims he or she has a new insight, new teaching, new truth that the church has missed for the last two thousand years. We must beware of anyone who claims that justification does not mean God declares us morally right with God. We must beware of anyone who denies that Christ has given to us 100 percent of His rightness (righteousness) and that we are in Him now.

Prominent voices in the church are preaching that the historic doctrine that Christ died in the place of sinners is closer to the pagan ideals of an angry deity being pacified by a human death and is nonsensical. Beware of them.

We have had a string of leaders, authors, high profile and little-known worship leaders who have become apostate—they turned from historic Christianity. Some outright deny Christ as the true way God has chosen to engage His world. Others have been much more sly in their apostasy (to be apostate is taken from the word that means "deserter" or "defector," and it means someone who intentionally rejects their previous stated belief in Christ and leaves the Christian faith). Unfortunately, scores of young churchgoers are not believing they must be justified by faith in Jesus Christ's death on the cross because of those false teachings.

May I remind you that Paul wrote, "Once you were alienated from God and were enemies in your minds because of your evil behavior. But now he has reconciled you by Christ's physical body through death to present you holy in his sight, without blemish and free from accusation— if you continue in your faith, established and firm, and do not move from the hope held out in the gospel" (Colossians 1:21-23).

Jesus is the substitute for us. His blood shed on the cross—by that death He became the curse for us (Galatians 3:13)—is at the heart of grace. God gives us everything, because of Jesus' sacrifice, for nothing. Or as many ancient theologians said, "Grace is God's unmerited favor." To reject the gospel preached to Abraham, seen in the four vignettes we looked at, is a perversion or subversion of vital grace. False teachers are dogs, but there is another dog to beware of.

For years suspicion was a major theme of my inner thought world—a suspicion that God was not for me. Oh I knew He "loved me" because I was told He loved everyone. But did He really like me? The dominating beliefs of the former life—that I must make my life work for me—was the base note of my existence for many years. And the contract I had with God, namely that He had done His part and I was to do my part, constantly reminded me how much I failed to keep my part. Grace was always available to others, but not to me. The Evil One would regularly condemn, "And you call yourself a Christian. A good Christian would never do that."

In his sinister way, as we saw already in the backstory from Genesis 3, his lie that separated Christ's love from the rules kept me in bondage to the rules, not to the God of love and grace. The Evil One deceived me into looking at God as the law giver who wanted to control my life with a myriad of new rules and not as a loving Father who wanted to free me from my enslavement to my self-reliance. Grace was for getting saved (I had already done that), but not for daily living.

Beware of that dog in your heart. Do not rely on your ability to follow the rules or put confidence in your self-indulgence. "That dog don't hunt," as Southerners might say. And that dog does bite.

We need to know that God's grace is real, deep, and given freely, not because of something good in us, but because He *is* love. We must dismiss our sneaking suspicion that God is against us and know "we are blessed along with Abraham" because to the degree we are unsure of grace, we will be enslaved to our former life, as it is the only way we know to live.

Getting an Accurate View of Love and Grace

In the cultural shift we have today, we need to have an accurate view of God's unearned love. These days it's popular to say, "God loves me just the way I am and He wants me happy, so I can be anything I want." While God does desire your perfect happiness, His love will not let you be whatever your heart wants to be if it is taking you to a place that further ruins who and what you were meant to be. He loves you contrary to the condition of your self-bent heart. In love, He says, "I have chosen you before you were born to be beautiful and blameless in My sight—righteous—to be My adopted child in accordance with My pleasure and will—to the praise of My glorious grace, which I have freely given you in the One I love, Jesus" (Ephesians 1:4-8).

As Paul engaged new followers of Jesus in a new church founded in Asia Minor, he pleaded with them to consider Abraham: "He believed God, and it was credited to him as righteousness. Understand, then, that those who have faith are children of Abraham. Scripture foresaw that God would justify the Gentiles by faith, and announced the gospel in advance to Abraham . . . so those who rely on faith are blessed along with Abraham, the man of faith" (Galatians 3:6-9).

Vital grace is about the good news, the bad news, and the very good news because it is about Jesus Christ. If the stories in the Bible are left as only stories about other heroes and how we should copy their lives, rather than as pointing to Christ, then we will either be loaded down with guilt and shame because we know we cannot live up to their level of spirituality and faithfulness or we will be filled with arrogant pride and self-righteousness because we know we are doing better than the characters' lives we are reading.

However, when we understand the stories as pointers to the person, life, death, and resurrection of Jesus Christ, we learn to hope and see how vital grace works and that we get everything for nothing. We are given what Christ has done and is doing for us and we find our place, our story, in light of His work. Our personal stories begin to make sense. Our relationships become more robust. Our mission in work, business, and with neighbors become connected and meaningful and our spiritual center with God is renewed. You see, it's one thing to say, "You should be more loving and forgiving because God wants you to and it says so in the Bible." It is quite another thing to explain how Christ's love and grace actually help us want to love and forgive and empowers us to love and forgive. There is a big difference in trying to be like Christ and living in Christ because of grace.

Vital grace isn't about what you have to do to rescue yourself. It is what God has done to rescue you. Where are you most likely to question your rescue? When you have failed? When you have lost your way? When life is complicated, hard, and you are suffering under pain? You will not rest in God's vital grace if you secretly think He is mad at you or live with the continual inborn suspicion and fear of His displeasure. However, when you look by faith to the Jesus of Abraham, who is the father of all who live by faith, not by the sight of human eyes, you will discover His love and grace, and hear the joyous words of the Father, "You are my beloved child and I like you."

FOUR

Ball and Chain:
The Power of Your Former Life

*Do not forget the covenant I have made with you, and do not
worship other gods. Rather worship the Lord your God...
However, they would not listen, but persisted in their former practices.
Even while these people were worshiping the Lord, they were serving their idols.*

2 Kings 17:38-41

Lee, a businessman with whom I had become friends, had grown up
in a traditional and strict Christian home. When he was nine years
old, he "walked the aisle and asked Jesus to forgive me of my sins."
He and his little brother lived in what they assumed was a stable
home until the day when he was just about to turn twelve. That's
when his dad left and his parents divorced. It was a crushing blow to
his tender heart, though he told me he had not been particularly close
to his dad. The Liar whispered into the ear of Lee's soul, *You had*

better learn to rely on yourself. After the divorce, money became tight at home, forcing his mother to take on two jobs.

Lee went on the graduate from a Christian university. He married a strong woman, also from a Christian home, and they worked in Christian ministry. He followed the typical path of a pastor, working as a youth minister for a few years, assistant pastor in two churches, and then the lead pastor in a string of small, independent churches. For the most part he worked hard to keep a disciplined, secure lifestyle, following all the accepted rules. But small churches did not pay enough to provide for the needs of his growing family, so Lee left the pastorate and moved with his wife and two kids to find new work in the marketplace.

Lee thrived in sales. He was charming, gregarious, funny, and excellent in communication skills. He finally had the stability and financial security he longed to have. Lee was "whole," or so he thought. Sales was a tricky business, so Lee switched companies almost every year to try to earn more. He always reasoned that it was his primary responsibility to provide for his family and that was why he was working so hard. Even though he sang "Indescribable" or "Great Is Thy Faithfulness" each week in church and admitted that he had Jesus, at his core, what he really wanted more than anything was financial security.

Unfortunately, his twenty-six-year marriage ended when his wife finally said she could not continue to live in the whirlwind of insecurity as he chased his real love, money. During the next year, he landed another top sales job and made gobs of money.

I do not want to make simplistic the complexities of the human heart, but in Lee's life, the damage of the sin done to him, and his believing the lie that *you cannot rely on God and better rely on yourself* became the base note of his entire life. God loved him and he knew that. But the god of his story was to gain security in his world and the way he chose it was through money.

That's the problem of our former life. We sin all the time because we suffer the effects of the ruin, or the fall. We are born spiritually dead. Have you noticed that you continue to struggle with certain temptations? Have you ever asked yourself, "Why do I continue to sin in my particular ways? Why do I seem to go back to the very things I want to be rid of?" You promise yourself and possibly others, "I will never do/say that again." Yet there you go . . . again.

For us to understand what the apostle Paul refers to as the "former life" and how that can affect us in the present, we need to grasp our backstory, that former life, and apply grace with its intended freedom promised. Paul reminds us, "You were taught, with regard to your former way of life, to put off your old self, which is being corrupted by its deceitful desires; to be made new in the attitude of your minds; and to put on the new self, created to be like God in true righteousness and holiness" (Ephesians 4:22-24).

Paul boldly told the believers living in the city of Corinth that their former lives were what they used to be but now they had new lives: "That is what . . . you were. But you were washed, you were sanctified, you were justified in name of the Lord Jesus Christ and by the Spirit" (1 Corinthians 6:11). He went so far as to call their former life a life in darkness: "For you were once darkness, but now you are light in the Lord. Live as children of light" (Ephesians 5:8).

If we do not deal with the motivational structures or the core of our lives, if we do not get to the thing that is really driving us and functioning as the true-life operating system, then progress in the Christian life will be an ongoing experience more like the movie *Groundhog Day,* in which we wake up every morning and continue in the same old patterns prior to conversion.

Creating Idols

Only about fifteen years after Jesus Christ ascended to His throne, Paul wrote a letter to Christians living in the region of Galatia who had allowed false teachers into their churches. In it he asked, "Formerly, when you did not know God, you were slaves [literally, devoted] to those who by nature are not gods. But now that you know God—or rather are known by God—how is it that you are turning back to those weak and miserable forces? Do you wish to be enslaved by them all over again?" (Galatians 4:8-9). We all can go back to our former lives. Do we really want to waste our whole lives, even after being "born again," in the chains of sin? Living under the power of our former lives is enslavement.

Have you ever considered how the ruin in your backstory has affected and shaped you in how you live now? If you are not familiar with the concept of life idols (false gods), it means that we make things in this world, even good things, central to our lives. We try to make them the "hero" of our stories and expect our idol to rescue us and give us life.

In my book *Gospel Coach,* I present four major idols of the heart: power, approval, comfort, and security. These idols are usually "good" things that have been elevated to the "most important" things.[1] There are many good things about finding approval by having a good reputation at work. Wanting to live in peace with others in the neighborhood is a Christian virtue. Working to build a secure financial future for retirement is a good thing. But do not misunderstand the key idea of idolatry. Those things, though virtuous, have the power to become *the* thing.

British pastor and writer Martin Lloyd-Jones wrote, "The greatest danger confronting us all is not a matter of deeds or of actions, but of idolatry. . . . What is idolatry? Well, an idol can be defined most simply in this way: an idol is anything in our lives that occupies the place that should be occupied by God alone. . . . Anything that holds a controlling position in my life is an idol . . . it moves and rouses and attracts so much of my time and attention, my energy and money."[2] The Lord had clearly commanded everyone made in His image, "You shall have no other gods before me. You shall not make for yourself an image in the form of anything in heaven above or on the earth beneath or in the waters below" (Deuteronomy 5:7-8).

The ancient teaching tool, *The Heidelberg Catechism*, a teaching aid German and Polish theologians wrote in 1563, declared, "Idolatry is having or inventing something in which one trusts in place of or alongside of the only true God, who has revealed himself in the Word."[3] Evidently the problem of idolatry has been around a long time!

One thing is certain. God will not bless a life in order to fulfill our own idolatry. No matter how good the idol may be (a good marriage, perfect kids, hard work, church work, or a healthy community growing in the knowledge and grace of Christ). God takes second place to nothing, because He is great, good, and gracious.

To keep away from our false heroes, we need to identify those things that are in the human heart. Somewhere along the backstory of our journeys, we learned and adopted a way to make life work out and to make things right again. Our world is filled, and always has been, with an assortment of counterfeit ways to find life.

We begin to adopt our belief systems through hearing words of affirmation or condemnation from people close to us or by watching others find success or make mistakes. We might get ideas from reading books or watching movies and television. Many of us heard stories of family members or experienced them while growing up with siblings who pointed us one way or another.

These experiences, along with the predisposition of our own personalities, shaped us and we "exchanged the truth about God for a lie" (Romans 1:25). Our search led us to find some way to achieve a sense of personal peace and comfort, to be accepted and approved by ourselves or others, and to have security from harm in order to justify our very existence. We foolishly swapped the Creator God for things in this world (see Romans 1:23). You and I have both done this.

The Bible says that when we are not living by the Spirit—not living by grace—we are living by the "flesh": "Those who live according to the flesh have their minds set on what the flesh desires . . . the mind governed by the flesh is death . . . it does not submit to God's law, nor can it do so" (Romans 8:5-7). Used in this sense, the flesh is the outworking of the driving force of the soul, mind, and heart of the person. The activities of that "heart" reveal our motivational reason for living.

Surface Idols

Paul wrote that the actions of the sinful flesh (Greek word is *sarx*) are "obvious." You can see them operate. My friend Dick Kaufmann coined the term, *surface idols*. The specific actions may be different in each person, but they *are* in each person. They rely on these things to provide meaning. Dick Keyes, director of L'Abri Fellowship, suggested, "All sorts of things are potential idols. . . . An idol can be a physical object, a property, a person, an activity, a role, an institution, a hope, an image, an idea, a pleasure, a hero."[4]

Our North American culture celebrates three primary surface idols: money, sex, and fame. Are they not obvious? We can see how money has become a powerful tool in politics, religion, war, medicine, government, all the way down to petty street crimes. Who doesn't talk about what they would do if they won the lottery? Can we see it in our own lives? Yet, while some people say money isn't important to them, the things that money can provide—a certain kind of car, house, boat, clothes, or holiday—are. Money is a big deal. A friend told me once that the people in his neighborhood all wanted to "retire before they retire."

And what about sex? We need not look any farther than television to see that sex sells. Sex has even received its own civil right. It is celebrated and championed. If someone challenges the "god of sex" in culture, they receive the full force of retribution.

Fame, unlike the other two, is more subtle. One may not seek national fame but loves a simple bit of notice within a small circle of friends, family, or coworkers. Many crave, through their social media, to receive some level of recognition. Some may want to be famous through music, Hollywood, politics, business, design, or even ministry, while others choose a quieter platform, such as "Teacher of the Year" or "Best Mom in the World." Some people would rather be famous for murder than not famous at all. You don't have to go to that length to want to be famous. You can exchange the word *murder* with almost anything else.

People can rely on many other surface things in hope of rescue. For one person their house is a surface idol. For another, a sports team. Some may idolize their grandkids, while for others it can be about finding love or having a child. It could very well be central for someone to have a great reputation among colleagues. Or perhaps they long to find life in their body shape or physical beauty. And some people overly focus on their career or title ("I am a doctor" or "I am a part-timer").

I have also known many church people who looked for life and gloried in their obedience to God's laws, Bible memory, theological correctness, or denomination. They may have begun their new lives by faith in Christ, but they continue to live with self-effort, works-oriented practices just as they did in their lives before Jesus. This is why grace in our hearts does not stop at conversion.

Church people are not the only ones who find life in their religious observance. Secular people have a set of beliefs they live by and that defines them as well. Vital grace is necessary for a nonbeliever to be made alive again and for the believer to *continue* to live in Him (see Colossians 2:6).

Another way to examine the surface idols of our lives is to "define for yourself a 'little hell.' For you, hell is being poor; for you, it's being ugly; for you, it's being fat; for you, it's being unloved; for you, it's being underappreciated. The fear of your hell compels you to choose for yourself a false savior god to save you from that hell."[5]

You might sing to Jesus, "I need Thee every hour," but beneath that what you wrongly believe is the need for a different lover, more money, new career, bigger house, or nicer car. Perhaps you sing beneath the Sunday songs, "I need my wife's respect," "my husband's affection," or "my parents' approval." We can see the surface idols of needing others to make us feel better (being dependent) or the need to be needed (a codependent). What do you see about your life? What is driving your behavior?

Source Idols

The "former life" is a lifestyle of the flesh. Fundamentally, it is the way we are motivated to make ourselves right again (to justify our existence and find life). However, if we stop at the obvious behaviors of our flesh (surface idols), we will not experience freedom promised by grace. Those surface idols are like fruit on a tree, not the roots of the tree. We must find out the *why* of our behavior by asking, "*Why* do I find I want to do the wrong things?" The truth is we are always controlled by our deepest passion, by what captivates our hearts the most. We must dig down to the motivational level through the application of vital grace. What are the foundational idols we are centering life on?

The heart has to have something to center itself in because it's the way we were made. As we have seen, God made us for connection with Him and with others. In that perfect garden, our first parents knew the very essence of comfort, security, and approval. But because our parents accepted the lie of the Evil One to rely on themselves, to find life outside of God (to be their own god), their thinking and ours became futile and our foolish hearts were darkened.

It has been said that Martin Luther, one of the early grace guys wrote, "The sin underneath all our sins is to trust the lie of the serpent that we cannot trust the love and grace of Christ and must take matters into our own hands."[6]

We now worship, serve, and center our lives around created things rather than the Creator (see Romans 1). At the risk of over-simplifying the complex world of our idol-making hearts, I would suggest we end up with three primary false idols or heroes:

> *Approval* (i.e., the belief that I am whole when either I approve of myself or others respect me, approve of me, and grant me worth) because we feel "naked and ashamed."
> *Comfort* (i.e., the belief that I am whole when I am experiencing personal peace—my little piece of heaven—and a chosen quality of life) because we live in a hostile and harsh world and life can be crushing and hard.
> *Security* (i.e., the belief that I am whole when my life and/or those I love are secure or safe in this world) because we are insecure because of our guilt, being cut off from God our Creator and others.

These three "source idols" are the roots of the tree and are what we're hustling to make us truly live and, from them, give life like roots of a tree to the surface idols we see.

Nineteenth-century Scottish pastor Thomas Chalmers had a penetrating insight to the human condition. He said, with my paraphrase:

> One may stop overeating but it's because a more mature taste has brought it into subordination. One may stop sexual lust, but it is because money is now what is its center desire. Even the love of money can cease to have mastery over the heart because it is drawn into the thrill of politics or business and now there is a love of position. But there is not one of these transformations in which the heart is left without an object. Its desire for one particular object is conquered—but its desire to have some object is unconquerable.[7]

Controlling sinful passion is not a matter of the will but the heart. The person who can first understand the heart and then control the heart can control every area of life.

Diagnosing the Source

One of the ways we learn more and more about vital grace in our lives is to understand how our non-graced lives actually work for or rebel against our rightness most days. We must understand how the ruin both in the Bible's story and in our real time story has affected us. If we are being controlled by our deepest passion, and we are, then we need to know what is really going on inside the heart.

Nobody understood the inner workings of the human heart better than Jesus. People of His day, like ours, put a premium on outward appearances. Our pop-media-driven culture makes heroes out of performance, money, fame, or outward beauty and cares little about character, unless you violate *their* standard of character. One of the things Jesus' enemies hated was that every interchange they had with Him led to the matter of their hearts. Jesus did not care how much they gloried in their public prayers, tithed, quoted Scripture, or even how preposterous their moral lives had become. He said once, "The things that come out of a person's mouth come from the *heart,* and these defile them. For *out of the heart* come evil thoughts—murder, adultery, sexual immorality, theft, false testimony, slander" (Matthew 15:18-19, emphasis added). Jesus was saying, the activities of the flesh are flowing from the inside.

From our beliefs (or what we are relying on to give life), we act accordingly. Again, Paul explained that those activities are obvious, we can see them, but what is on the inside is more difficult to determine. We may not see in our hearts what we are relying on, but we can see how they are working themselves out. Everybody does what they love to do, and what they love is in their hearts. Everything follows the heart.

The "heart" (*kardía*) is mentioned more than eight hundred times in the Bible but is never used in the literal sense of the muscle that drives the blood. That is, "heart" is only used figuratively, as the *affective* center of our being and the *capacity of moral preference* (*volitional desire* or "*desire*-producer that makes us tick"[8]). It is the motivational center or our "desire-*decisions*" that establish who we really are and what we are actually relying on in this life.

The longing necessity of the human heart (the center of our personal being and motivational structure of life) must have something to build upon. That is why God repeatedly told us to guard the heart. Our beliefs drive our behavior.

You may have sung, "Christ is enough for me, everything I need is in you" last Sunday, but when you headed off to work the next day, all bets were off because what you "really" needed was a sale. You might have to stretch the truth to a client to make that sale. The "stretch" is a sin, but there is something beneath that is more important. It is the sin beneath the sin.

Or you may be a mom who will not correct your children because you say it's harmful to their personalities. Beneath that statement and practice, however, you may really be living for your own comfort because the daily struggle of the crying, whining, or defiance is just too much to correct. It is easier to tune it out than keep up.

It will not be enough simply to exhort a man with a "don't lie" rule or preach a sermon on the virtues of sexual purity. Appeals to the will, no matter how valid, may achieve some degree of moral conformity, but they will not go far enough to unearth and tear down the deep source of idolatry compelling you to rely on your former life: one built on false idols for approval, security, or comfort in this world.

Let's go back to culture's surface idols, in particular the three we discussed earlier, and explore what is beneath them. You are part of the culture and, in reality, it is your former way of life. Because of vital grace, you have a new life. Nevertheless, you constantly wrestle with the pull and temptation of the former life. We all do.

The first one is money. On the surface, money can become a god in this world. Jesus talked about money more than He talked about heaven and hell combined. You see, one person may live for money but what he or she really lives for is the sense of approval, self-validation, and identity it provides.

However, for another it may provide financial security. Remember Lee? The Liar promised if he pursued money or, as he rationalized it, "provide for my family," he would be secure. His surface idol, money, was his way to serve his source idol, security, in his traumatized, insecure world. Yet for another, money provides them the god of comfort in their soul as their labors or investments provide for a comfortable lifestyle.

Jesus explained that it is impossible to serve two different "gods": "No one can serve two masters. Either you will hate the one and love the other, or you will be devoted to the one and despise the other. You cannot serve both God and money" (Matthew 6:24; Luke 16:13).

Here Jesus had just told His followers not to store up treasures on this earth, but to store them up in heaven—a future: "Where your treasure is, there your heart will be also" (Matthew 6:21). Notice, what you are living for, in your heart center, that is where you will use your money because what you treasure is in the heart. Jesus wasn't against wealth, but He was against making money the thing you use to find any sense of comfort, approval, or security, which serves as a substitute for Him. Money is as big a deal today as it was then.

The second is sex. Jesus Himself repeated the Old Testament's "Do not commit adultery" command, which included *any* intimate relationship outside of marriage—including having sex with someone unless you are married to that person.

Yet we live with the cultural consensus now that if you are not having sex with someone, married or not, you are a weirdo. It is the norm in culture, and it is abnormal to believe that it could be a bad thing. It is "just sex," our culture demands.

However, it isn't "just sex." Both experientially and existentially, deep down, you know the truth. Something happens between people when they connect at a sexual level. It completes or complicates relationships.

If you are divorced because your spouse committed adultery, you know it was *the deepest sense of betrayal*. If it's "just" sex, why was it not just like they shared a pizza in the break room at work? If it is just a physical thing, what's the big deal? Why did it break up the family and ruin the kids? Why are so many adults still bruised and wrecked over what a parent or relative did? Why do so many have regret or bad memories of the people in college? Why are so many people dealing with guilt and shame through antidepressants? You get the idea. Sex is powerful. Sex isn't a sin, but the misuse of sex is and there is a fake god beneath it.

After reminding us not to misuse sex, Jesus expanded on it to include lusting after someone else. But He did not use a sexual term for "lusting," He used a word used for desire or longing—the biblical word *coveting*. He meant what a person truly yearns for or sets their inner being on. Literally, He said to "*greatly desire* to do or have something." Though the word can be used both in a good way and in a bad way, in this instance it means an over-desire or inordinate desire that is all controlling.

Here is why sexual idolatry is the former life. We have a new life that was bought by Christ and given freely back to us, by God's free grace, so we are now connected to Christ. We belong to Him, body and soul (see 1 Corinthians. 6:13-15, 19-20; Ephesians 4:17-24). But we must not deal with sex at the surface level. We have to go to the source, because what controls the heart when it comes to sex (the source idols) are the same as all other surface idols.

When we are challenged to turn from our former lives in the way we live sexually, we have to answer the questions of motivations: Is this one of those areas where we seek approval, security, or comfort? Is there some place of security we are wanting? Is it our personal comfort we are really after? Or are we motivated by the approval or desire of approval from someone else or from a group of people?

The third surface idol our culture worships is fame. Most people, truth be told, seek some level of acclaim or recognition. It is more prevalent than the desire for power. In fact, God warns us about not trying to steal His glory (honor, splendor, fame, and dignity) more than trying to assert power (see Isaiah 42:8). Fame and the closely associated word *glory* are surface idols that long for our attention to make a name for ourselves. God is very jealous for His glory and His name.

Though not everyone desires to be a celebrity or famous, most of us do want to be admired and/or recognized by others through some accomplishment. Some find it in work, some in family, some by their beauty, some through music, some by their art. Others work hard religiously to be recognized. With the help of the internet anyone in the world with a computer or smartphone can have fame. Obviously, being admired isn't a sin. But the sin beneath seeking our own glory or fame is that through it, we think we will find self-actualization, inward peace (comfort), or personal safety (security).

Why are you seeking to be known or achieve fame by something in this world? Is it the path to personal security or approval—even if it's self-approval? Once again, the deeper root system of the heart is the issue.

Our source idols, the ones deep in the heart, offer promises to make us comfortable, and provide us with meaning, security (completeness), and own our "shalom" (personal peace, wholeness) if we follow after them. All through life we are evaluating the good and bad responses we are getting from those choices.

When we experience a good or effective outcome for following our source idols, we reinforce the idol. But these same idols also threaten that if we do not serve them, our lives will be ruined, meaningless, and empty. We begin by expecting them to serve us or provide for us, but they eventually overtake us and master our very lives.

John Calvin, a leader in one of the greatest spiritual movements in Christendom, used the term *fabricum idolarum*, which is a Latin for "a maker of idols or a place where idols are mass-produced." What we make, we think we own. What we think we own, we think we control. However, we actually work hard to control what we think we own, only to discover control is an illusion.

The Move to Control

When we wrongly believe our source idols (heroes of our stories) can give us life, we continue to live under their works-oriented promises. Then when we experience an ineffective outcome, we may change direction or try a new approach. When the source idols are threatened (we think that we are losing our approval, comfort, or security), we struggle to manage life in order to gain or regain control. In this sense, control is not an idol, but the means by which we try to order our lives to function according to our belief in what will complete us. When idols fail us or are under threat of being removed, in order to regain or keep control, we resort to one or two possible methods in our pursuit: control by force or control by manipulation.

Control by Force

We gain or regain control by use of force or violence, which moves along the spectrum depending on how well we get control. Again, Paul said that this behavior was obvious to see. It can move from having a harsh attitude to threatening people with harsh, hateful words that bring "discord, jealousy, fits of rage, selfish ambition . . ." (1 Corinthians 12:20). *The Message* translates the idea, "Cutthroat competition . . . divided homes and divided lives . . . the vicious habit of depersonalizing everyone into a rival" (Galatians 5:20-21).

If getting control back that way doesn't work, some people step it up to abuse. Again, we are told to get rid of "fits of rage," "dissensions," "factions," a brutal temper, backbiting, anger . . . (Galatians 5:20; Ephesians 4:31) all the way to threats of harm, even physical attacks, or murder ("get rid of brawling, slander, and every kind of wickedness, ruthlessness, and murder").

Control by Manipulation

Some people use a different tactic to gain or regain their sense of loss of control in keeping their idol alive and well. They use manipulation. Again, imagine a spectrum. On one end they may use overindulgence of others with feigned praise. They over-use flattering words or offer promotions, rewards, or treats to others in hope to regain control of them or the situation.

There is a difference between someone using compliments versus flattery. Flattery is over-the-top praise with the hidden motive of advancing a personal agenda. Paul reminded one church that he never used flattery to control them (see 1 Thessalonians 2:5).

The writer in Proverbs warned his reader to be on look out for a woman who uses her flattery (Proverbs 6:24) and when people use flattery, they are simply "spreading nets" (a trap) for their neighbor (29:5).

On the other end of the manipulation spectrum, people use deception by lying, hiding motives, telling half-truths, and/or hustling the other person to get what they want ("falsehood," "empty words," "swindling," or misusing their sexuality).

In these ways, using violence or being manipulative, people try to keep their idols alive and well. Power or control is not an idol but it is the way we seek to maintain the "blessings" the idols promise and occasionally provide.

A member in a men's group I once led, Russ, shared that his wife told him early on in their marriage that if he ever cheated on her, she would divorce him, take him for everything he had, and be certain he never saw the children again. The other men chuckled, feeling perhaps a shared sentiment. He and his wife didn't realize it, but they were both living in the flesh.

She didn't have a control idol, but she was trying to use a combination of threat and manipulation to maintain the control of her security idol. Wanting to have a solid marriage that included a husband who didn't cheat on the marriage was a good thing, but her security was not to be found in his faithfulness, but rather in Jesus' faithfulness for her. And Russ, out of his desire for personal comfort (not wanting to "get into it with her"), never told her that it wasn't a loving thing to say nor a reason for him not to stray. They both wanted good things, but the center of life is not in creating their own security or comfort.

If violence or manipulation continue to fail as a way to keep control, we may try to escape the reality of soulish emptiness through some other way. In this case, we begin to live below the line of despair. When life becomes too overwhelming, some people escape through the "deaths of despair." Sadly, since 2014, millennials have seen a 47 percent increase in major-depression diagnoses. Deaths of despair (dying from suicide, alcohol, and/or drug overdose) increased in the millennial population in the last ten years.[9] And the trends continue at an alarming rate going forward.[10]

Peter reminded the Christians scattered across Asia Minor that they spent enough time in the past (their former lives) doing what pagans choose to do: living to get drunk, partying, engaging in orgies (extreme indulgence in sexual pleasures), carousing (uncontrolled and uncontrollable addictions), and practicing detestable idolatry (1 Peter 4:3). It is a life of futility and ruin.

In the movie *Fellowship of the Ring*, based on J. R. R. Tolkien's book of the same title, Gandalf met with Bilbo Baggins, a hobbit, right after his 111th birthday party, when Baggins was about to leave the Shire for good. Gandalf wanted to know what Baggins planned to do with the ring he had. "What about this ring of yours, is that staying too?"

"Yes, it's in an envelope over there on the mantelpiece," Bilbo replied, adding he planned to leave it for his nephew, Frodo. At the same moment, though, he pulled it out of his pocket and began to stroke it, looking at it as something of great beauty and value. "Why shouldn't I keep it?"

When Gandalf suggested he leave it behind, Bilbo reacted in a burst of anger. "Now it comes to it, I don't feel like parting with it. It's mine, I found it, it came to me!"

Gandalf, surprised by the heated expression, responded, "There's no need to get angry."

But Baggins shouted back, as he continued to caress the ring, "Well, if I'm angry, it's your fault! It's mine! My own, my precious."

Gandalf was stunned. "Precious? It's been called that before, but not by you."

Now, in a full rage, Baggins put up his fists at Gandalf and screamed, "What business is it of yours what I do with my own things! You just want it for yourself!"

What an extraordinary example of the power of "our precious" or the thing we rely on to give us life. The ring, even though Baggins had carried around in his pocket and used it to do tricks for his amusement, did not raise its clinging lust for him until it was threatened. He thought he owned it, but alas, when he realized he was to lose it, he resorted to control. First, he lied. He told Gandalf that he placed it on the mantle. When Gandalf suggested he give it up, his next response was to lash out in anger, threat, and a readiness to punch Gandalf. He tried to use power to regain what he believed he was losing.

This story can be replayed over and over from parents who lose their tempers with their kids who won't do as they are told, to the politicians who lie to their constituents to keep the security of their office, to me being impatient with traffic because I'm concerned with my own comfort. It is the lifestyle of the flesh, relying on our own version of approval, security, or comfort from the things of this earth. It is our "former life."

The story of Bilbo Baggins and the ring doesn't end, of course, with that interaction. Gandalf responded with the loving strength of a friend's rebuke. Baggins wept, and they embraced. Baggins agreed to let go of the ring, gathered his things, and headed to the door. But Gandalf stopped him as he called out, "Bilbo, the ring is still in your pocket." Bilbo pulled the ring out and stared at it, then slowly allowed it to slip off his palm, landing on the floor with a heavy thud.[11]

Trusting in our material-world heroes or idols is a daily struggle, not a one-time event. It holds a sturdy grip on us from as far back as our childhoods. It is our former lives.

If you are a Christ follower, God gave a very clear and profound call to your life, namely, you are not to make for yourself an idol in the form of anything in heaven or on the earth or in the waters below. You are not to bow down to them or worship them. The thousands of people racing through the airports, the people sitting in the eight lanes of traffic, or the neighbors at the ballfields and frozen yogurt spots are not exempt from this warning.

Does the King who made everything we see, as well as what we cannot see, care whether we replace or reduce Him in our lives? He does care, and the main reason is because *He is the highest Good in the universe.* He created you to experience your greatest good and highest joy; to know astonishing acceptance and deepest sense of community; to live securely, all by connecting or centering lives, in worship of all Sovereign, mighty King, who created and sustains all things. To reject Him by trying to replace Him or reduce Him with a fake is to bring a curse, disaster, or ruin on life.

If you are not in Christ, the lifestyle of the flesh is all you have in this world. It is not your former life, it is your present life. Sure, you can experience seasons of the fulfillment of approval from others (your parents, a boyfriend, or boss), or security (job, financial, or career path), or comfort (a sense of personal peace or a measure of affluence). But if you dig deeply enough, one day you will see that whatever "it" is (the thing you are really living for, centering life on to grant you fulfillment), owns you and you are actually enslaved to its controlling power over you.

As followers of Jesus, those who are in Christ, the life of the flesh, our former life, cannot be ended by telling ourselves, "It's no way to live." It cannot be stopped by fear of punishment. It cannot be suspended by quoting the rules of the church, society, religion, or even the Bible because the heart wants what the heart wants. If you are not a Christian, it is the only life you have and you will not give up it. If you are a Christian, there is a better way to live.

The good news of God to humanity is that He made a new and different way by His amazing vital grace. We no longer have to live enslaved in a lifestyle of the dead but can own freedom in life. The gospel of vital grace is the only solution to find true and lasting approval, comfort, and security. Jesus, as our Prophet, has given us the only approval we need.

We are completely accepted by the Father through the satisfying work of Jesus. He has declared us forgiven and accepted us as daughters and sons. As our Priest, He cleanses us from the sins of our former life and provides us with the true comfort our hearts and lives need.

When we are hurting from our own sin or from sins committed against us, we can go to our Priest Jesus and find renewal, care, and renewed strength. As our King, He has purchased our complete security and freedom, both here and into eternity. There is no one else, no other hero to our story than King Jesus. He alone rescues and renews.

FIVE

What is True Spirituality?

*He has rescued us from the dominion of darkness
and brought us into the Kingdom of the Son He loves,
in whom we have redemption, the forgiveness of sin.*

Colossians 1:13-14

During most of the earliest days of my Christian journey, I tried to find a way to manage my sin instead of believing that Jesus really had forgiven all of my sins "in accordance with the riches of God's grace that he lavished" on me (Ephesians 1:7-8). I had hoped, like so many others, to find the formula or secret to living the new life. I have a library full of books from many different perspectives on how the Christian life is to be practiced. I suspect you might as well. Not only have many books been written on the subject, but millions of sermons have been preached to multimillions of Christ followers on it. It is in understanding and working out of our salvation that we want to unpack.

Even Paul wrestled with this idea of living the new life and shared about his own struggle:

> I do not understand what I do. For what I want to do I do not do, but what I hate I do. And if I do what I do not want to do, I agree that the law is good. . . . For I know that good itself does not dwell in me, that is, in my sinful nature. For I have the desire to do what is good, but I cannot carry it out. For I do not do the good I want to do, but the evil I do not want to do—this I keep on doing. (Romans 7:15-16, 18-19)

Have you ever had that inner dialogue? I guess the real question is, how often do you have that thought? Paul added, "What a wretched man I am! Who will rescue me from this body that is subject to death?" (Romans 7:24). Did you notice he did not say, "What formula is there for me to get out of this repetitive cycle of returning to my old life—the former way I lived?" Know why? Because there isn't a formula, prescription, or "mechanical solution to true spirituality."[1]

It has been my experience, both personally and in community with other men and women, that we are His (and that nothing will change that), and that the path to follow for life in the Spirit is a long and difficult one. How does God's free grace, once given, apply to life going forward and produce life change? Amid his own struggle, Paul noted that it isn't a "what" but "Who" that delivers us.

Instead of a prescription to living this new life, let's consider how the reality of vital grace and its power to give profound freedom works out in our lives.

The Pursuit of Identity

The life of vital grace begins with true Truth, a firm belief that what God has said about Himself, about us, and about His creation is real and trustworthy. If we "begin with the end in mind" we discover all of creation and our existence are made to enjoy life with God and others. The essence of getting right with God is that we actually "get God." As John Piper wrote, "Nothing is going to bring satisfaction to [our] sinful, guilty, aching hearts besides God."[2]

One of the most pressing issues of our day is one of identity: Who am I? It is one of the earliest questions we ask of ourselves. It comes before, "What should I do with my life?" Sometimes we try to answer the "who" with the "what," but we know deep down that "what I do" is not "who I really am."

Years ago, it was common to hear someone say "He is on a journey to find himself" or "She needs to go and find herself." I heard a celebrity pastor say rightly that before you can determine what you will do with your life, you need to decide what you will be. What kind of person will you choose to become? You need to decide what values you will live by. Another preacher rightly said that your identity is found in your adoption as a son or daughter of God. That is true as well. At least partially anyway. You won't be who you were meant to be or do what you were designed to do if you don't know who you are and whose you are. This is critical to true spirituality.

You may have thought, *If anyone knew what I've done in my life, they would turn away in disgust.* But Paul wrote that anyone (the despicable, the disgusting, and the morally upright) who repents and relies on Christ is given a new identity "in Christ," wherein he or she is a new creature, regardless of how corrupt, decadent, or morally zealous the old creature was in Adam (see 2 Corinthians 5:17).

Who you were was a spiritually dead person because you were holding a birth certificate with Adam listed as your father. Your old identity in Adam, the first man we saw in the backstory who disbelieved and disobeyed God, needed to die and be reborn. When the miracle of being spiritually reborn happened to you, you became a new creation; old things (who you were in Adam) passed away and all things became new. You have a new identity. Who you are now is proven by what God has said about you, not by your performance— either immorally or morally.

So where do we often look to find our own personal identity? Allow me to suggest three alternatives common to our current life this side of Eden.

Culture

Our culture is pressing on us every day a way to achieve our identity. The consensus says that we are only natural, that we can live as if this world is all there is. The shout of the culture shapers is that we are self-made, and that our personal identities can be achieved as we embrace their social-political cause (left or right), financial class, or sexual determination. In other words, we achieve our identities by embracing their cultural expectation or social construct and become part of the larger cultural identity.

Family

Our families can raise us to achieve our identities by embracing the traditions, race, or nationality we are born in. Mostly in traditional, non-Western culture, the role in family (the family name, honor, identify with "my people") is about shaping an identity. You may have been raised with a family heritage, race, nationality, or an expected career that was impressed upon you as the most important thing that identified you. Perhaps even being in a Christian family, the family name and honor actually superseded your Christian faith.

Inner Desires

Our own inner desires work to achieve a sense of personal identity. We believe the often-told lie that we can be anything we want to be. In the educated West, we are individualistic and cheerfully own our expressive individualism by being our "authentic self." We get to be the hero of our own story in a sense. We are told that everyone decides their own truth of their own personal identity, based completely on their own desire. In fact, one of the highest moral ethics flowing from self-determination is that we have to be true to ourselves and follow our own dreams. It comes to us as subtly as, "You can be anything you want, so follow your heart." That comes from the false starting point that we are the captain of our own lives because there is no Creator. The idea that we are self-made is in media, television, movies, and music. But it is a lie. "You can be anything you want to be" and achieve your identity by your efforts promotes a self-oriented life that leads to disaster.

Many of us may be looking to achieve an identity through how we live as parents, through our moral conformity, by our degrees in education, or by our careers. Those are things we are doing, but they wrongly substitute for *who* we are. Ultimately, those things are only attempts to try to achieve our identity through our performance. And any identity we have to work to *achieve* leads to enslavement. If we look to our careers to find our identities, we are slave to that career to name us. We often introduce ourselves by our careers (I am a lawyer, a sales manager, mechanic, engineer, etc.), but if we lose that role or job, have we lost ourselves? Some people do because they were a slave to that role or career. People are putting themselves into unrepayable debt to achieve an identity based on their degree from a certain university. Debt is a form of slavery.

You Need an Identity that Is Received

If you are in Christ—if He is not just an add-on and you're not trying to use Him to achieve your goals, but rather He is the center of your world and rules your life—understand, He will determine what you do and who you decide to be. Moreover, your identity in Him will determine who you become, what you do, and who you decide to do life with. If you are a follower of Jesus Christ, your core identity is invaluable in developing a healthy view of life and is crucial to enjoying life with God and others. True identity must be received, which means it comes by grace—something given to us, not by us working to achieve it.

We begin life in vital grace by a belief. However, our starting point is from the gospel story. Since we all live according to our beliefs, it is essential that we have an accurate belief—a "true Truth," not just our own personal truth. We are transformed by our thinking or belief center (see Romans 12:1-2). We are to be transformed by what is true Truth.

The truest thing about you is what God has said about you, and that Truth is found in the gospel story God told. Do you remember how our story begins? Remembering is vital to understanding grace in life. That's what will allow you to be confident that an all-powerful (God is great), all-knowing, all-glorious God, who is personal, relational, and all-loving (God is good), is your Father. For "God created mankind in his own image, in the image of God he created them; male and female he created them. God blessed them" (Genesis 1:27-28). Instead of us saying we self-identify, we can confidently say we have received our "God-identity."

The roots of vital grace will grow deeper as we understand the reality of our true identities. There are three pivotal concepts that make up our true selves: (1) our lives as created by God; (2) our kinship in Christ; (3) our life callings as disciples. Once we grasp these important concepts and how they weave into the very fabric of vital grace, we are better prepared to withstand the hardness and storms of life and can begin to make great strides forward with clarity and purpose. Any confusion or misunderstanding of our identities and how these three components interweave to form them will tend to hinder us being strengthened by grace in day-to-day living.

Let's explore what I have come to see as three integrated aspects to our received identity. They are integrated in ongoing movement, not linear like 1, 2, 3. And if we want to live in vital grace, we will integrate our received identity into our ongoing lives, day by day, moment by moment. These three aspects are creatureship, kinship, and discipleship. I am intentionally using words that are somewhat unfamiliar to us because I want the idea to be new and different.

Creatureship

One main element of our received identity is our *creatureship*. Jesus Christ created us, and all things seen and unseen (see Acts 17:24; Ephesians 2:10; Colossians 1:15-16; Revelation 4:11). As we found in the backstory of the gospel story (see chapter 2), we are in the imago Dei. We are not a cosmic accident or "oops baby." We are quite intentional. God said, "Let us make mankind in our image" (Genesis 1:26). The gospel story revealed in the Bible is a challenge to the atheistic/naturalism and polytheism (many gods) belief systems in our world and is one reason why the false teachers (deconstructionists) attack the Bible's authority so vigorously.

The Greeks (polytheists) created gods in the image of humans; their gods had many good and evil human qualities. Today, the educated West does not accept what the majority world, in the majority of time, has believed—that there is a Creator (or creators) of things.

However, we can trace our identity to the gospel story. Christianity gives us an identity story. It is a coherent story. A cohesive story. A compelling story.

Jesus Christ, the true Eichon (image) of invisible God created you (see Colossians 1:15-16). As you consider your true origin, you discover that God created you for community (to be in relationships), with the highest dignity and value as male or female, with meaning and purpose to co-manage or care for His creation, and with real, everlasting beauty as one deeply connected to Him. You were made with unique gifts, abilities, desires, and an eternal soul. You have transcendent meaning and real purpose to your existence. The greatest meaning is found in getting God. We are the completion of His creation, and He affirmed it by saying it is "good." Does this change the way you see yourself? *This is good news!*

Your created identity is invaluable in developing a healthy view of life and crucial to enjoying life with God and others. As theologian Michael Horton explained:

> We come to know ourselves as human beings—that is, as God's image-bearers—not only by looking within but chiefly by looking outside of ourselves to the divine Other who addresses us. It is only as we take our place in this theater of creation—the liturgy of God's speaking and creaturely response—that we discover a selfhood and personhood that is neither autonomous nor illusory but doxological and real. Who am I? I am one who exists as a result of being spoken by God.[3]

You won't be who you were meant to be if you don't know who you are. What is your starting point in your identity?

My friend Corey Jackson told me about a conference he attended where the keynote speaker opened his session by playing a word association game with the two thousand-plus attendees. He began, "I am going to say a word and you respond back, out loud, with the first thing that comes to mind." He paused, then said, "Human Beings."

With a roar of one united voice, the crowd yelled back, "Sinners." That is remarkably sad.

Now if you were raised in a conservative churched home, they might have mitigated the phrase, *You are a sinner* with *but saved by grace*. I don't know what word you thought, but that is *not* how your life story begins, because that is not how the gospel story begins. You are made as an image bearer of God.

Think about this: Which is more compelling to say to a little child, "You are a sinner" or "You are good and can be anything you want to be"? Is it any wonder we are losing this generation to a story that has as its starting point an appeal to our self-oriented life? We have a greater, more compelling, and cohesive story, and it begins with the personal, all-glorious God making us with transcendence, wonder, and greatness. Let the One who made you, not an impersonal chaotic universe, define you.

In the historic Heidelberg Catechism, the writers asked:

> What do you believe when you say, "I believe in God the Father almighty, Creator of heaven and earth?" That the eternal Father of our Lord Jesus Christ, who out of nothing created heaven and earth and everything in them, and who still upholds and rules

them by His eternal counsel and providence, is my God and Father. I trust Him so much that I do not doubt that He will provide whatever I need for body and soul and will also turn to my good whatever adversity He sends me in this sad world. He is able to do this because He is almighty God and desires to do this because He is a faithful Father.[4]

When I was in graduate school someone wrote on the chalkboard (yes, I am that old), "God does nothing except in answer to prayer." The next morning, we noticed someone had written beneath it, "What about creation?"

The entire throne room of heaven worships God with songs of His creative wonder: "You are worthy, our Lord and God, to receive glory and honor and power, for you created all things, and by your will they were created and have their being" (Revelation 4:11). And His creative wonder extends to you: You are "fearfully and wonderfully made" (Psalm 139:14). To the degree that grabs hold of you, as you see the grace given in creation, it will transform much in life. But it is not the only part of your identity you need to allow to shape you.

Kinship

A second key element or component of our identity is our *kinship*. Even though we were created by God, our first parents ruined it all. Our image is marred, and we are born spiritually cut off from God and others. Our history is replete with twisted, broken relationships. There are people who hurt us and others we hurt. There is a long history of man's hatred toward others, suffering under the wretchedness of racism, war, and injustices. Individuals suffer the horrors of murder, rape, slander, anger, etc.

We don't need to go deep into ourselves to find how each of us is personally ruined. Some of us suffer under a torturous sense of shame for what a perceived loved one did to us. Some still struggle with nagging realized guilt for our own selfish choices. No one is immune from a fear of loss, fear of disapproval, potential poverty, and sickness. Add into the ruin that our work is messy and hard. Our sense of meaning in the universe is now made up of whatever gives us purpose or money or experience. We have lost all sense of transcendence (something or someone bigger and grander than ourselves). When spiritual death came into the world, the judgment of God (or alienation) became real and we know it.

But you were rescued by Christ. We saw in Chapter Three that Jesus came on a mission to rescue His children who had been taken captive and enslaved by their own self-oriented choices. Let me give you a new identifier—*kinship*. You are God's kin. You are rightly related to Him by a new bloodline. You are now "in Christ." Paul used that term "in Christ" more than seventy times to describe a new element of our identity.

Consider the following key realities of our kinship: that in Christ you have been made complete! (see Colossians 2:10). What can be added to someone who is complete? We are connected to and in union with Jesus. That completeness is assured because *Christ reconciled us to God* (see Romans 5:10; Colossians 1:20, 22). God is no longer against us because God Himself closed the gap.

In your former life, you were alienated from and an enemy of God.

But now, you have been reconciled, and God has made peace with you: "Since we have been justified through faith, we have peace with God through our Lord Jesus Christ, through whom we have gained access by faith into this grace in which we now stand" (Romans 5:1-2). You have complete acceptance and everlasting security. You have "standing" with Christ because you are reconciled to the Father through Him.

Vital grace tells you that Jesus Christ came to do for you everything you need to get God. You see, if you have your own set of beliefs, rely on yourself, or have tried to live up to the moral standards others have demanded, to do or not do, you are still trying to achieve identity. The joy of vital grace is that God has made peace with you. The question in old western movies to the villain facing the hangman's noose on whether he has "made peace with his Maker" isn't the real question. The real question is, "Has God made peace with you?"

Completeness in Christ is also secure because Christ is the only Substitute we need. Substitution is the heart of the gospel of grace. The core of your sin is substituting yourself for God, and the essence of salvation is God substituting Himself for you. As reformer Martin Luther wrote, "The genius of Christianity takes the words of Paul 'who gave himself for our sins' as true and efficacious. We are not to look upon our sins as insignificant trifles.

On the other hand, we are not to regard them as so terrible that we must despair. Learn to believe that Christ was given not for [petty] and imaginary transgressions, but for mountainous sins; not for one or two, but for all; not for sins that can be discarded, but for sins that are stubbornly ingrained."[5]

Jesus, in dying in our place, became the perfect atoning sacrifice for your sins (1 John 2:2). In being physically resurrected back to life, He justified us—declared us not guilty (Romans 4:25), conquered sin's controlling power (Romans 6:8-12), and gave us a new desire (2 Corinthians 5:17) and a new power to live for our new desire (Romans 6:12-14). Grace not only saves us with an everlasting salvation, it also gives us a nature that delights in everything that is of God because it is a divine nature (2 Peter 1:3-4).

Part of our true identity is that Jesus has done everything we needed to be acceptable and accepted with God. Here is a reality in life: to make something clean, something else has to become dirty. Your dishes, the floor, the countertops, a nine-month-old face after eating spaghetti, or the diapers afterward. Here is another reality: you can't declare yourself clean or not guilty.

You sinned against others, yourself, and God and became unclean or morally dirty. Something else must clean the dirt. This is exactly the great news we need to hear: "God made him who had no sin to be sin for us, so that in him we might become the righteousness of God" (2 Corinthians 5:21). Grace is not a commodity we traffic in; God's grace is Christ.

During the self-esteem movement in the early 1980s, which has since metastasized into our culture of entitlement, it would be common to hear in sermons, books, and songs that "you are worth so much, Jesus gave His life for you." Indeed, we are created image bearers of God, but we have selfishly rebelled and been utterly ruined. If God found your soul worth dying for because you were so lovely or so great or so remarkably wonderful, how glorious is grace? Again, it's what you achieved. If you had a loveable status, then there is no need for free grace.

In Romans 5, it is a misunderstanding Paul is careful to correct: "Very rarely will anyone die for a righteous person, though for a good person someone might possibly dare to die" (v. 7). He chose two words—*righteous* and *good*. By righteous he meant someone who is innocent. By good, he used a word that means intrinsically good, that is by nature. Eugene Peterson translated the idea, "We can understand someone dying for a person worth dying for [e.g., an innocent person], and we can understand how someone good and noble could inspire us to selfless sacrifice" (MSG).

Paul then extoled the wonders of God's amazing grace. He did not say Christ died because we were good, worthy of great value, or wonderful. His death was never about the goodness of man. Instead, Paul reminded that Christ died for "the ungodly" (v. 6), for "sinners" (v. 7), and that we were God's "enemies" (v. 10). That we achieved a status worth dying for is a subtle and deadly dilution of God's grace. God's grace is about the greatness of Jesus Christ not about our worthiness.

Another standard sermon line is, "Jesus loved you so much He died for you." That makes no sense without some context. If you were sitting on a bench viewing the Grand Canyon and someone walked up to you and said, "I love you so I am going to die for you" and then jumped off the cliff, what sense would that make? Jesus' dying for you and me makes sense only if there was a death required of us. And there is, because of our sin against Him. That sin requires a payment, namely death. Only then does substitution make sense.

As C. S. Lewis observed in *The Weight of Glory*, "God did not die for man because of some value He perceived in him. . . . To have died for valuable men would not have been divine but merely heroic; but God died for sinners. He loved us not because we were lovable, but because He is love."[6]

Jesus died the death that was rightfully mine. He became the judged, paying the complete debt for sin I had with God because He is great, not because I am great.

We are also complete in Him because God has adopted us as family. Adoption is making us His children by free grace. Notice in the following passages how often we are told it is all of God:

> The Spirit you receive does not make you slaves, so that you live in fear again; rather, the Spirit you received brought about your adoption to sonship. And by him we cry, "Abba, Father." . . . We are God's children." (Romans 8:15-16)

> God sent his Son, born of a woman, born under the law, to redeem those under law, that we might receive adoption to sonship. . . . God sent the Spirit of his Son into our hearts . . . and has made you also an heir." (Galatians 4:4-7)

God did it all and we received it all.

Have you considered the innumerable implications this reality can have on a life? Jesus gave up His name and laid aside His reputation when He went to the cross. By His resurrection and ascension, being given the name above every other name, He has removed our shame of being nameless orphans in this world and given us His name.

By His grace, He transformed who you were naturally into a supernatural person (2 Peter 1:4) with God as your Father. Jesus Christ, God the Son, is your Elder-Brother. The Spirit of His Son brings you restored honor by admitting you to all privileges of being an heir of all the promises and a co-heir of all His inheritance (Romans 8:16-17; Galatians 3:29).

We must continuously realize the cost of our rescue, being captivated by the love, beauty, and freeness of His grace: In love, He predestined, justified, and glorified. In love He predestined us to be adopted as sons and daughters" (Ephesians 1:4-5). Not that we loved God, but that He first loved us. That reality should take our breath away. Think about this: "This most generous God . . . gives you something you can then give away, which grows into full-formed lives, robust in God, wealthy in every way, so that you can be generous in every way, producing with us great praise to God" (2 Corinthians 9:10-11, MSG). We are God's "kin," or rightly related to God by His new bloodline with kinship wealth that we are to give away!

Discipleship

The third element or reality of your identity is your discipleship. I know most of us do not think of being a disciple of Jesus Christ as forming our identity, rather it is something we are to do. However, understand that from the moment you were rescued, the Holy Spirit is now discipling you in your Christian journey. You are being renewed by Christ. Discipleship is progressive work of God not something static or something we do. As Stephen Smallman wrote,

"A disciple of Jesus is one who has heard the call of Jesus and has responded by repenting, believing the gospel, and following Jesus, *with others*."[7]

Discipleship is about progressively changing from one way of living to another, and it happens by the active involvement of the true accountability partner, the Holy Spirit. Jesus prayed to the Father to give us the Holy Spirit (the Spirit of Truth) to live in us forever (John 14:16-18). That is how Jesus can promise, "Never will I leave you; never will I forsake you" (Hebrews 13:5).

The Holy Spirit does many things for us. One of them is to point us back to Christ (John 16:12-15) and convince us the gospel is true and real. He also convicts us, leading us to joy-filled repentance. We are also renewed in His power to follow after the Lord, and He works in us the change we need to complete in us all that the Father had originally designed us to be: "God's love has been poured out into our hearts through the Holy Spirit, who has been given to us" (Romans 5:5). It is through the active working presence of the Holy Spirit that we become both gospel-influenced and gospel-influencers in the world.

Why do we need the active working presence? One of the chief reasons is that we are both saints and sinners simultaneously. Not sometimes I am a saint or sometimes I am a sinner. The Holy Spirit's disciple-making plan involves reminding us of our saint-ness. We are united and complete in Christ. God has given us everything we need for life and living as a God follower. That is why we are regularly referred to as "holy saints."

Yet we have to be aware of the proclivity we have to doubt God and to disobey what God clearly shows us is the way He wants us to live in unity with Him. The Holy Spirit keeps aligning us to His ways, to overcome the temptation to return to our former way of life. There is coming a time, it might be in the near future or may have already come, when life is going to seem impossible and you will want to slip back to your old habits of relating to this world, to others, and to life's stressors. You are going to think, *I should just go back*, either to the old pleasure-seeking ways or to the religious rules.

One of the loving things the Spirit does is to remind us, "I have been crucified with Christ and I no longer live, but Christ lives in me. The life I now live in the body, I live by faith in [Jesus Christ], who loved me and gave himself for me. I do not set aside the grace of God" (Galatians 2:20-21). He keeps us from going back.

When you are unclear about the reality that at the same moment you are a saint, complete in Christ (reconciled, adopted, united with Him), and still someone who can fall away in one moment of your choosing, you will struggle to get free rather than be free to struggle.

If you forget you are a sinner, you may be devastated by your sinful behavior because you have too high a view of yourself. When you forget you are a saint, you have too low a view of yourself and may live in the shadows as an orphan. Both are true at the same time. This is a reality of life in vital grace. It is a key part of our discipleship—following Jesus in life.

One day you will become what God fully intended you to be at the beginning. God's intention in making you like Christ is to be as He is, the perfect human. Jesus was, in human flesh, the true Image of the invisible God, and His desire is for you to be fully human as an image bearer. You are not able to change your past, but God will change the future that your past was taking you to.

Your spiritual and emotional health is consistent with the degree you have believed the true Truth in vital grace and are integrating it into your life. Culture may tell you that you alone are the hero of your own story, but I suspect you have discovered that is an empty promise. In fact, that is what most of us are being told every day: *Look deep within and find your inner strength.*

The world tries to make you believe that as you find your personal independence you will discover your personal freedom and strength. Vital grace points us to what is true: the more you depend less on self and more on Christ, the freer and stronger you will be.

Because you are changed from an old identity into a new one by God's grace, you have a new future. You now enjoy a renewed freedom to be who you were meant to be. We are not simply following the teachings of Jesus, which makes us Christians. We are united with Christ. We are not our own, but He is in us and we are in Him, forming true spirituality as fully, accepted, secure, and at peace.

Discovering Real Love

Once we are secure in our understanding of who we are in union with Christ as created, rescued, and discipled people, we are placed in a profoundly new place in life. Grace not only forgives our debt, it also takes us into a new life with a renewed and higher calling.

Here's the thing: Some in the Christian world think that once you say God wants something from you, you have distorted grace. They say grace is free and therefore we are not in debt to God. They stumble on two classic hymns: "Jesus Paid It All" with the stanza, "Jesus paid it all, all to him I owe"[8] and "Come Thou Fount," with the lyric, "Oh to grace how great a debtor daily I'm constrained to be."[9] Indeed, those lyrics might make us think that we are to pay him back by being a good person. Of course, we could never pay God back. More importantly, He does not ask us to pay him back. As Paul joyfully promised, "There is no condemnation for those who are in Christ Jesus" (Romans 8:1). We have been gifted everything we need, freely.

Jesus was asked one day, "What is the most important thing God wants?" Basically, what's the main thing? We might think of many answers. He wants our worship. He wants us to do what He asks. He wants us to pray. He wants us to care for His creation. He wants us to glorify Him. He wants us to practice mercy and justice.

Jesus replied with as clear an answer as you could get: "Love the Lord your God with all your heart and with all your soul and with all your mind and with all your strength. . . . [And] love your neighbor as yourself. There is no commandment greater than these" (Mark 12:30-31). This statement has been called the Great Commandment, but the two commands cannot be separated. They are not sequential on a list like, "God is first, neighbors are second, and you are third." The two are equal in importance. We are to love God and at the same time to love neighbor. When I love my spouse, my children, my neighbor, I am loving God. I love God by loving my neighbor, who is also imago Dei.

The main thing God created us to be was a whole-hearted lover of the God who is love and to love those who are made in His image. Because we are the imago Dei of God, it is right and good to love Him. Is "owe" Him really too big an expectation?

Later, when He was alone with His closest friends, Jesus made a qualitative edit to the command. Just after washing His disciples' feet, He told them, "A new command I give you: Love one another. As I have loved you, so you must love one another" (John 13:34).

We are to love God and others as Christ has loved us. Paul pressed the thought later: "Follow God's example . . . as dearly loved children and walk in the way of love, just as Christ loved us" (Ephesians 5:1-2).

Paul also exhorted us to "let no debt remain outstanding, except the continuing debt to love one another, for whoever loves others has fulfilled the law. The commandments, 'You shall not commit adultery,' 'You shall not murder,' 'You shall not steal,' 'You shall not covet,' . . . are summed up in this one command: 'Love your neighbor as yourself.' . . . Therefore, love is the fulfillment of the law" (Romans 13:8-10).

Steve Brown, from whom I have learned more about free grace than anyone else, commented on this passage, "You owe love . . . it is an obligation. And there are no exceptions to this either. You owe love to the unlovely, to the mean and to the unattractive. What if someone doesn't love you back? You still have the obligation to love. What if someone doesn't want you to love him or her? You still have the obligation to love."[10]

Certainly, God does not owe His grace to anyone. What could God owe someone who has nothing or to someone who is dead, with no spiritual life at all? But do we not owe God eternal gratitude? Not owe in any sense of paying Him back, since as we said, He doesn't want to be paid back, even if we tried. Gratitude, though, isn't a payment, is it? Honor and thankfulness are not forms of paying for a debt. Those are a rightful and glory-giving responses to the kindness given. We must be careful that a hesitancy to say we owe God nothing keeps us from worship and proper response to grace. Remember, we are by nature people who are ungrateful, which is why Jesus warned His followers about being ungrateful: "Jesus asked, 'Were not all ten cleansed? Where are the other nine? Has no one returned to give praise to God except this foreigner?'" (Luke 17:11-19).

About twenty-five years ago, I heard a story about a woman who married a man she didn't know well. After returning from their honeymoon, her husband handed her a list of duties he expected her to do for him—how he wanted his meals prepared, his laundry washed and folded, and the house cleaned. It was a shock to her, but she was young and didn't know any better. She tried hard to love him well and serve him by doing the things on his long list. He wasn't harsh or violent, but he did have high expectations.

One day, after about ten years into the marriage, he died of a heart attack. It was sudden and unexpected. She lived as a widow for two years. Then one day she met someone, fell in love, and remarried. Her second husband loved her and did many kind things for her. He told her how much he loved her and how beautiful she was. They laughed a lot and found enjoyment in being with each other. Several years later while cleaning out old boxes, she found the list of duties from her first marriage. She smiled, then laughed. Everything on the list she was still doing. But now, she did them not out of duty but out of love.

When we are transformed, rescued, and made His followers we receive a new heart with new motivational structures to love God and our neighbor. We also receive a new power to actually do it.

Your understanding of living in vital grace will never be greater than your grasp of this reality: you have been given a new heart. Your former life as a child of Adam and Eve is dead. Christ now is alive in you, and through the power of the Holy Spirit, you are free to love.

We have the delight of finding in Him, our forgiveness. And, through Him, we can offer forgiveness to others who are still struggling to forgive.

You can only love to the degree that you have experienced love. Only for the heart that has been absolutely loved and knows absolute forgiveness, can you love God and your neighbor. Only through an experience of vital grace through Jesus Christ can the heart be supernaturally changed to love those who wound. Someone noted, "Religion says, 'God will love us if we change.' Christianity says, 'God's love changes us.'"

If you have ever tried to love the way Christ has loved you, however, you know you have come face-to-face with the realization that you cannot do that. It is a hard discovery to admit that you cannot love God or your neighbor the way Jesus did. The writers of the *Oxford Book of Prayer* understood what has to happen in our lives if we are to love well. They reminded us how we need to pray for love: "Dear Lord, I know that if I do not love you with all my heart, with all my mind, with all my soul, and with all my strength, I shall love something else with all my heart and mind and soul and strength. Grant that by loving You first, I may be liberated from all lesser loves and loyalties and have You as my first Love, my chief Good, and my final joy."[11]

In the next chapter we will consider what we do once we are certain of our union in Christ and His will for us to love Him and others. One thing I know for certain, if you are someone who has experienced God's love and have received everything from God for free, you now want to please the God who has loved you and given you everything. Your will has been radically and miraculously changed. If moralism or self-hedonism drives you—the sense that you have to earn God's favor through your obedience, have to work to pay Him back, or wish to continue to rely on yourself, living as you choose—then you may not have experienced a radical outpouring of God's grace. Because when you do not get grace, you end up following rules made by others. Or worse, you give rules to others.

I have a friend who is an expert model car artist. He builds 1/43-scale model cars for collectors and enthusiasts all over the world. He is one of the top-two model makers in the industry. A long time ago he began what would become a great skill in modeling by refurbishing automobiles. Soon after completing a total rebuild of a 1959 Triumph TR3, someone stole it. He filed a police report but never heard anything. More than a year later, he saw a sale ad for the same car in a city some two hundred miles from home. He had really enjoyed his, so he decided to go and look at the one listed, thinking he might buy it. When he arrived, though it was a different color and had different wheels from his car, he thought it was similar enough that he wanted it. So he bought it.

One day while working on the car, he noticed a mark on the frame and laughed out loud. "No way." The mark he saw was the same he had made on his car while rebuilding it. He told me later, "I built that car, and I bought that car."

Here's the point. God built you to be His, but you, as your parents before you, did not want God. You wanted you. Your life was stolen, ruined, enslaved, and living under a curse. God's grace in His gospel is that He loved you, came after you, bought you, pardoned you, and put into your life all His excellence. He is rebuilding you to ultimately find life with Him. You are at the same moment accepted and acceptable, but He hasn't stopped loving and working to renew you and all things. In fact, one day He will come back and complete the renewal.

SIX

Amazing Grace Land

*Grace not only saves the soul with an everlasting salvation,
but it also imparts a new nature that delights in God.*

Unknown

In our culture there are a few stories from the Bible from which we hear common sayings. When a person in the office is fired for a failure of someone higher up, people say, "He [or She] was the sacrificial lamb" (taken from Leviticus 16). Typically, when we have predicted a bad future for someone, like knowing a friend's new marriage isn't going to last, and the prediction comes true, we might say, "Well, the handwriting was on the wall" (taken from Daniel 5). And the common phrase used when someone helps a stranded driver or takes care of a stranger in need is that the person was "a good Samaritan" (taken from Luke 10:25-37).

Jesus told the parable of the good Samaritan to a man who asked, "What must I do to inherit eternal life?" His questions raised an issue about his eternal destiny or, in essence, "How do I get accepted by God?" Imagine that. The man asked the One who promised eternal life how to get it.

Jesus answered by first addressing the man's surface idol, probing to find the hero of his story. "What is written in the Law?" Jesus replied. "How do you read it?"

The dedicated religious leader responded with the same answer we observed from the man who wanted to know what God expected from us, "Love the Lord your God with all your heart and with all your soul and with all your strength and with all your mind" and "Love your neighbor as yourself."

Jesus, as before, responded, "You got it. Do it and you will experience God's gift of eternal life."

But the man wasn't happy with the answer. He wanted to "justify" himself, not excuse himself, and be able to declare himself not guilty of any law breaking. He displayed the problem every human heart has: we want to find some way of self-justification, to declare ourselves not guilty and instead, be all right.

Jesus responded, as usual, with a parable. Parables were concise stories that had a central truth. This parable was not a story to discuss the need of mercy ministry or social justice, as important as they may be. In fact, the specific features of the parable are not central to the point. Remember, it did not actually happen and there was no real Samaritan. It is only a story to explain to the man how he could be made right with God. That is his central heart issue: how he will earn eternal life (justify himself) by observing a strict moral code.

Jesus turned to His audience and began His dramatic parable: "A man walked down the hill on Jericho Road and was robbed, beaten, and left for dead. Two Jewish leaders who said they loved God and loved others came by, but they wouldn't help." (Here Jesus subtly pointed out that the law-abiding way cannot make us right with God, because we cannot do the law, no matter how good a rule keeper we think we are.) He continued, "Then a Samaritan came by, saw him, treated him, and took him to a roadside tavern. He stayed up all night caring for the wounded man and then paid for two months of lodging with a promise that when he returned, he would pay whatever else was due."

It was a generous love beyond belief. Not a reckless love, but planned, purposeful, expensive, and undeserved. It was something for nothing. The generous Samaritan loved the stranger, the neighbor, and his enemy (Jews hated Samaritans), rescuing him from certain death.

Remember, in response to the law to loving one's neighbor in order to get life, the man had asked, "Who is my neighbor?" Jesus responded with a question of His own: "Which one of the three proved to be a neighbor?" In other words, who loved? Jesus was working on the man's heart to pry away his self-righteousness. It isn't "Who is my neighbor?" but "Am I a neighbor who is loving to all, including my enemies (the Samaritan)?"

The man begrudgingly answered, "I suppose the one who showed mercy."

And Jesus, with a certain degree of pathos in his voice, said, "You go love like that and you can have eternal life." Let's be clear, Jesus was not suggesting an alternative method of salvation. He was working on the man's personal, hidden idolatrous heart. The man was seeking his ultimate approval by his own works. Jesus was exposing his source idol. What was he really relying on for approval from God?

Now, what should have been his response? Plainly, it should have been, "That is impossible. I cannot do that. No one can do that. I cannot even love myself like that! And you are saying I must love everybody like that. I am more like the person in the ditch, helpless and in desperation. Lord, have mercy on me, a sinner. I need grace." Had he responded that way, Jesus would have said, "Exactly. I am the True Good Samaritan. Believe in and rely on Me and I will give you the life you so desperately need because that life is a gift of grace not by your effort."

When we realize we are to love God and love one another and admit we cannot do it, what can we do? The work of God's grace does not diminish the call to a dual love—to love God and love neighbor—it actually enlarges its call on us because the call is not to do external expressions or do some good deeds. Grace does not "let us off the hook," as it were, so we no longer have to love God or neighbor, nor is it an expectation to try harder to be morally superior by adding greater effort. Grace allows us to love God with wholeheartedness and to love neighbor with the kind of love Christ has given us.

If we are loving neighbor—trying to act like a "good Samaritan"—because it gives us a sense of moral approval (we feel better about ourselves—i.e., self-approval) or so that the helpless "neighbor" or others will admire us (or we gain fame for the action—i.e., other-approval), it is not the true kind of love God is calling us to. It is serving our former life's idol of approval.

To have a dual love is our ongoing struggle in what the theologians call "sanctification."

How We Get Loving God and Neighbors Wrong

Sanctification is not just an appearance of transformation (outward moral conformity) but real transformation, making us into the likeness of the True Man, the perfect Man, Jesus Christ.

But how does moment-by-moment change happen so we love God and love neighbor? The reality is, sin has caused a deep injury to our lives—and by us to others' lives—and we are in need of daily renewal to regain the marred imago Dei.

In your past, perhaps you were taught a two-dimensional way to change your life: "Trust and obey for there's no other way." To trust, you were told each and every Sunday to "accept Jesus as your Savior." So you prayed the prayer. But then the obey part came. It was up to you to just try harder, stop sinning, and do what God wanted. You were warned that if you didn't obey, you would hurt Jesus' feelings or make Him sad or, worse, make Him mad. Or maybe you were told if you disobeyed, you would lose His favor and no longer be His friend.

The first half of the dimension to "accept Jesus" was easy. The second half was way more difficult. As much as you thought you could stop sinning and love and obey God, you couldn't. I know too many who finally gave up trying to change themselves through will power and self-denial. They wore themselves out trying to be good enough and gave up altogether trying to live for Jesus.

This may be one reason many end up leaving their church. They say, "I really tried, but I just could never do what I was told every Sunday I was supposed to do." There is a big difference between striving to live for Jesus and living in Jesus.

Perhaps you were taught a one-dimensional approach—that faith alone (accept Jesus as your personal Savior) was the only dimension you needed. You learned, "You are under grace not law, so just surrender more to grace because there are no rules." Some even went so far as to teach that if anyone mentioned obeying God, they were being legalistic. Many have tried to live as if obeying God did not matter. In fact they lived as if God had not graced their lives at all. Grace wasn't vital to life because it did not bring any transformation. They remained in their former lifestyle. Grace did not uproot anything and bring new life, rather it gave them the ticket to keep living for themselves.

Another approach you may have learned is what I term the double dimension. Like the two-dimensional approach, the double dimension recognizes the need to believe in Jesus. However, the obvious reality is that Christians do fail all the time (we don't love God, our friends, spouses, kids, much less our enemies), so the second part was to repent again and again. The double dimensions are faith (accept Jesus as Savior) and repentance for sins. Perhaps you learned that those two are all you need to change. Trust Jesus and admit through confessing or admitting your sin and, by it, denying yourself more and more. This approach never invited radical transformation just admitting ongoing failure.

A young pastor received a letter once in which his mentor in the faith explained to him what the vitality of grace did in bringing about life transformation: "The grace of God . . . teaches us to say "No" to ungodliness and worldly passions, and to live self-controlled, upright and godly lives in this present age, while we wait for the blessed hope—the appearing of the glory of our great God and Savior, Jesus Christ, who gave himself for us to redeem us from all wickedness and to purify for himself a people that are his very own, eager to do what is good" (Titus 2:11-14).

In this letter from Paul to Titus, Paul offers three dimensions: confession of sin, believe on Christ, and obedience. Those are what sanctification works out in our lives and grace covers.

Vital Grace in 3D

In reality, there are three dimensions of vital grace renewing the life of a Christian. I have termed these dimensions "Gospel 3D." The three dimensions—distress (confession or repentance of sin), delight (faith in Christ alone), and direction (obedience to His call)—though different pieces, operate together in life as one. Gospel 3D is how we change, grow, mature, develop, or become sanctified as we walk along the road in the land of amazing grace. God's method of sanctification is not through self-reliant activity and effort (as in "Just try hard" or "Just say no") nor is it merely self-indulgent apathy (as in "Just let go and let God"). Rather, it is what Francis Schaeffer termed, a "moment by moment active passivity."[1] God's grace trains us with three ongoing dimensions or movements in life by the present activity of the Holy Spirit.

The Dimension of Distress: Joyful Repentance

One of the first elements of living moment by moment as a new creature is not only realizing you are still ruined and wounded by your sinfulness, but you ruin and wound others by your sinfulness. When you became a Christian, it is true you were forgiven and completely free from any debt with God, so why do you need to repent or confess your sin?

We are well aware of the fact that we continue to commit sin. All Christ followers go back to their "former" lives. And repentance, confessing our sins to God and others we have sinned against, is crucial in keeping the vibrancy of our lives in the Spirit and friendship with others. Martin Luther reminds us, "Consequently one ought to be disposed to say, 'It is true. I have sinned. But I will not despair on this account.'"[2]

When repentance is active, we do not need to despair, but we are to be distressed by our sin and have a change of mind for the wrong direction we are heading. When King David was confronted with his sins against Bathsheba and her husband, Uriah, he repented to God, "Against you, you only, have I sinned and done what is evil in your sight" (Psalm 51:4). He had sinned in adultery and an orchestrated murder, but ultimately, he had sinned against God because he had looked to someone to find comfort in life and for personal security through a murder. He was deeply distressed because it was evil, so he repented from the heart, confessing to God.

But first he focused on God's kindness: "Have mercy on me, O God, according to your unfailing love; blot out my transgressions. Wash away all my iniquity and cleanse me from my sin" (Psalm 51:1-3). It was that kindness (God's unfailing love and the knowledge that he could be made clean) that brought David to repentance.

When we get to the place of repenting or confessing our sins, we are agreeing with God that we have been after ungodliness and an "over desire" for something other than Christ's sufficient life. As we repent, we are agreeing to live in reliance on the Holy Spirit. The Spirit assures us of our new life and makes us wholeheartedly willing and able to live for Him. He is faithful and true to restore and renew us. As Steve Childers explained, "So repentance should not be seen as merely changing our external behavior but primarily as a willingness to pull our heart affections and our heart trust away from our idols."[3] We are circling back to our truest selves: created men and women who have been loved so deeply, reconciled back to God by Christ's substitution, and adopted as co-heirs with Him.

The bent of the human heart is still toward self. We have an ongoing need to agree with God about our self-justification, self-protection, self-excuses, and self-righteous behavior.

Author Paul Tripp reminds us, "The problem is that sinners find confession difficult. We all have ways to take ourselves off the hook. When the light of truth shines on us, we instinctively deny, recast history, explain away, accuse, blame, defend, argue, rationalize, or hide . . . [but we should] speak humble, specific words of confession to the Lord, not weakened by "buts" and "if onlys."[4]

It's a reality we all must face, but the easiest person for you to deceive is you. Having a repenting heart toward God and others keeps you honest beneath the surfaces of life. It keeps you from self-deception. It will uproot the idols of your former life.

If you do not practice regular repentance of ongoing sin, then when you do sin (which you will), you will default to the bent of the human heart to either try to justify yourself—"He made me do it" or "It was a minor infraction, just a little mistake, and we all make them"—or you will try to correct your behavior by rededicating your allegiance to the God of law and rules—"I promise I will never do that again." Making excuses or rededicating yourself to the rules is a rejection of Christ as your loving, good, and kind God, offered to you in His gospel of grace.

Joy-filled distress in repenting or confessing your selfish, sinful doubts and acts of betrayal to God is not self-pity and self-punishment, it is admitting that sin has re-entered your life and you have relied on your former life's idols. The way back to the wonder of closeness and vibrancy of a restored friendship with the Father is through a door marked repentance. Repentance is naming the specific sin, not simply readmitting the obvious that you are a sinner.

We do need to repent to God our surface sins (i.e., confess the lie I told my parents or spouse), but joy returns when we can get to the sin at its source (i.e., the reason I lied was I trusted that my comfort and security would be found in what I lied about) and uproot that sin by relying on Christ. And as the apostle John promised, "If we confess our sins, He is loyal to His promise and always equitable to forgive our sins and cleanse us from everything that does not meet His approval" (see 1 John 1:9). As my friend Steve Brown reminds us, "Repentance simply means agreeing with God about what needs to be changed in your life. . . . It means nothing more nor less than agreeing with God about who you are, what you have done, and what needs to be changed."[5]

Many people in the coaching industry teach that coaches never tell, they only serve to mirror back to their coachee what is in them. They teach that the solution is in and of the person, so let them find it for themselves. Well, that might be a good thing if the person sees that, in and of themselves, "dwells no good thing." If God's mirror, the Bible and Spirit, causes them to confess their sin and selfish non-love, and repent by the joy of the gospel, and turn back in faith to God, then that is a good thing.

We must not try to divide repentance and faith up in some chronological order. That is why I said they are continually operating in us. Repentance must be connected with faith. We must repentantly believe and, as we will see, believe repentantly.

The Dimension of Delighting: Ongoing Faith

You may not agree with me on this, but having faith is one of the most misunderstood dimensions of living a true spiritual life. We understand that we are to believe, but what does it mean to believe or to say we have ongoing faith? Francis Schaeffer wrote, "Eve doubted God, that was her sin. She called God a liar. Eve doubted God, and I as a child of God am now to do exactly the opposite: I am to believe him. Eve doubted, and mankind in revolt doubts God. To believe him, not just when I accept Christ as Savior, but every moment, one moment at a time: this is the Christian life, and this is true spirituality."[6]

Trusting in Christ does not come natural; trusting in ourselves does, so life in vital grace is one of ongoing faith or delighting in the truth that Christ really is enough. If we re-read Titus 2, we see that grace teaches us to live in the present world "while we wait for . . . our great God and Savior, Jesus Christ who gave himself for us to redeem us" (vv. 13-14).

How do we learn to delight? It will be a challenge to delight in Christ so it will always be a fight to believe He is enough. However, doubt is not really the absence of belief, but actually a re-directed trust. As we have already seen, whatever our hearts cling to is what we are believing will give us approval, comfort, and security— basically life we lost in the garden. A. W. Tozer explains, "The roots of our hearts have grown down into things and we dare not pull up one rootlet lest we die."[7] For the Christian, doubting God is actually placing faith in someone or something other than the resurrected Christ and the promise He has given to be life to us.

My good friend and colleague Jim Moon, Jr. and I enjoy texting pictures of some of the common cultural sayings about faith we find in stores or restaurants or hear on television. If you have some of these hanging on the walls in your home, forgive me, I do not mean to offend. "Just believe" is the most common saying. At Christmas it changes to "Believe" or "I believe," in Santa, I suppose. Another one is "If you believe it, you can achieve it" or "If you put your mind to it, you can do anything." Believe "it" is a bit confusing if you try to unpack "it." If I believe I can win the lotto, does that mean I can win it? I haven't won yet!

We are often told it is the sincerity of our beliefs that matter. I have friends who earnestly believed they would earn a huge return by investing their retirement with a man they met at church. They believed him and his plan and sincerely trusted in the investment portfolio he sold them. They believed "it"—that they would enlarge their wealth. But the man was a scam artist and eventually went to prison for a pyramid scheme that took money from hundreds of other investors. Now my friends are broke. They sincerely believed "it" but did not achieve it.

Allow me to offer a few more: "Believe you can and you're halfway there"; "Believe there is good in the world"; "Believe in the magic"; "In this house we believe"; "She believed it, so she did it." You get the picture. Believing is a big thing. Everyone believes in something. You can choose what you will believe in, but you cannot choose whether or not you will believe.

Here is some good news: Christianity isn't a leap into some ethereal idea of wishing, no matter how sincere. Christian faith is never faith in faith nor is it "just believe." Unfortunately, in the Christian speak we use, our idea for belief can almost sound the same, with the change of a word or two. "God said it, I believe it, that settles it" is very common Christianese. "God helps those who help themselves" rings up there as well. A blend of human effort and God's help to make up for any short coming on our part.

Who are each of the versions pointing to? All of them, secular or Christian plaques, make us the foci. We are the ones who must believe it. Is the call for us to have ongoing faith to work up our own faith? I suspect you would agree with me that it's not. So what is the solution?

What do I mean when I say that faith is often misunderstood? It is critical we have the right understanding of faith, so we do not slip away into non-faith. We live in culture of doubt. Our neighborhoods are filled with cynics. Politics, science, and medicine can make us doubters. Our educational system breeds skepticism. Business leaders, corporate America, government, as well as our financial markets lead us to the belief that nothing around us is the sure thing, so we end up swimming in a sea of doubt.

The Christian faith is never without content. Many say, "We place our trust, our belief, our faith in God." But which one? Oh, "the God of the Bible," comes the answer. That's a start. But what specifically about God? "Oh yes, we must believe in Jesus," someone adds. Believe what though? "Well, we believe that Jesus died on a cross." Yes, but how many of the Roman soldiers who were at the crucifixion two thousand years ago believed Jesus died on the cross? All of them. So what do we have to believe about Jesus' death on a cross?

Read Titus 2:13-14 again: "Our great God and Savior, Jesus Christ, who gave himself for us, to redeem us from all wickedness and to purify for himself a people that are his very own." What are you to believe about Jesus? "He gave Himself for us." That is, Christ Jesus lived the life you needed to live perfectly—to love God and love neighbor—died the death you were supposed to die by giving His life as the judgment and was raised to new life as proof that the debt was paid in full (He redeemed you), purifying you as His very own.

Need more proof? The apostle Peter wrote, "He himself bore our sins in his body on the cross, so that we might die to sin and live to

righteousness; for by his wounds, you were healed" (1 Peter 2:24).
Paul also wrote:

> Consequently, just as one trespass resulted in condemnation . . .
> so also one righteous act resulted in justification and life. . . . For
> just as through the disobedience of the one man the many were
> made sinners, so also through the obedience of the one man the
> many will be made righteous . . . where sin increased, grace
> increased all the more, so that, just as sin reigned in death, so
> also grace might reign through righteousness to bring eternal life
> through Jesus Christ our Lord. (Romans 5:18-21)

A young woman said to me once, "I would believe in God if He
would speak to me Himself. I might even believe in Christianity if
someone came back from the dead to tell me about it." I replied,
"Someone already has come back from the dead, once for all time,
and God has spoken life through Him." Every promise God has
given is found to be true and it finds its yes in Jesus Christ (2
Corinthians 1:20). Moment by moment, faith in Jesus intersects with
our hearts at the deepest level.

How do you find the approval you so desperately need? You
believe that on the cross, Jesus Christ gave up His reputation, honor,
and name so He could give you a name, His name. He made Himself
nothing, taking the very nature of a servant and was obedient to death
on a cross. You rely on the truth that Jesus took every bit of your
shame, by being shamed on the cross. He was resurrected from death
and God exalted Him to the highest place and gave Him the name
that is above every name (see Philippians 2:7-11). He gave us the

final approval by His resurrection to the highest place. Our verdict is in. We have all the approval needed. "He is my son in whom I am well pleased" (Matthew 3:17) has been passed to us as His very own.

How do you find the sense of peace and comfort in life? You trust that Jesus came and gave up His position in glory, lost all His riches, so you could have the full riches of grace. You rely on the truth, as the Heidelberg Catechism puts to words, "that I am not my own, but belong—body and soul, in life and in death—to my faithful Savior Jesus Christ. He also watches over me in such a way that not a hair can fall from my head without the will of my Father in heaven: in fact, all things must work together for my salvation."[8]

Jesus ascended to heaven, and one of the reasons was to send us His Holy Comforter: "I tell you the truth—it is for your good that I am going away. For unless I go away the comforter will not come to you; but if I go, I will send him to you" (John 16:7).

How do you find your security in an increasingly insecure world? By faith in the revealed truth, that Christ surrendered His personal security, offered up Himself to sinful men to suffer, was put on trial, and put to death (even a shameful death on a cross) to guarantee your eternal security. He was resurrected from death and then ascended to the throne where He is the reigning King over all things, and you are a co-heir with Him. As Ephesians 2:4-7 says: "Because of his great love for us, God, who is rich in mercy, made us alive with Christ even when we were dead. . . . It is by grace you have been saved. And God raised us up with Christ and seated us with him in the heavenly realms in Christ Jesus in order that . . . he might show the incomparable riches of his grace, expressed in his kindness to us in Christ Jesus."

I once asked Chuck, a man whom I had just started coaching, "What is the present value of Christ's death and resurrection in your life?" His answer showed a transformed life:

> These last five years there has been great loss. Job loss, financial security, and marriage issues. I was unjustly ruined professionally. I suffered pain and doubted myself a lot. Questions like *Am I good enough? Strong enough? Smart enough?* constantly plagued me. Christ saved me from losing my faith. He saved me from materialism. He saved me from losing my marriage in pursuit of love elsewhere. In saving me, He gave me a deeper sense of joy and His love for me. He really is enough and everything I needed.

That is a life of ongoing repenting and believing.

The Dimension of Direction:
Open-Hearted Obedience

My close friend Dave had a serious heart attack and bypass surgery a few years ago. He had what the doctor called a "widow maker." In Dave's recovery, his surgeon told him that he had to stop eating fatty foods, start walking, and do a regimen of cardio exercises or he might not live long. Was that a power play or love for his well-being? I suppose Dave could have followed the doctor's directions for one of three reasons: fear of death, personal pride in his ability to regain his health, or out of a love for his family's and his well-being.

Our obedience is not the destination but *one* of the dimensions of our sanctification. We may choose to follow His direction (or the law He set up; that is His rule over us) in one of three ways: fearfully, arrogantly, or open-heartedly.

Fearful obedience. One motive behind why we obey can be because we are afraid. Many religions and a lot of Churchianity is fear-based in the way we are to approach God.

In the blockbuster movie *Braveheart*, the Scottish army under the command of William Wallace was soundly defeated by the British forces at Falkirk because of the treachery of Robert the Bruce, one of the main Scottish lords. The Bruce's father had worked out a private arrangement with the king of England to turn Wallace over to the British. Wallace discovered Robert was responsible for their routing. The Bruce was horrified and went to see his leprous father who had self-quarantined.

"It's what had to be done to protect the future of the family, increase your lands, in time, you will have all the power in Scotland," his father told him.

Robert the Bruce replied forcefully, "Lands, men, titles, power—nothing."

"Nothing?" his father snapped back.

"Yes, I have nothing. Men fight for me because if they don't, I throw them off my lands, starve their wives and their children."[9]

At any time in your life were you told to obey God out of fear that He would, as it were, "throw you off His land, starve your wife and children?" Far too many have lived in obedience to the rules because of their fear God will ruin them. Someone told me recently, "I always give my 10 percent tithe to God because I am afraid if I don't,

He won't bless me financially. And God has always kept His end of the deal." That is non-grace. I wanted to tell him, but didn't, that God didn't want 10 percent; He wants you to present your life as a 100 percent sacrifice to Him.

If you grew up in a church that practiced fear-based religion, I want you to know, they lied to you. Unless God's goodness and love is clearly established as the context for obedience, we will never obey from the heart because love is the motivating force of generous obedience. Knowing God's love is the one constant in all the inconsistency of our lives.

Arrogant (or proud) obedience. Another motive is pride. We strive to purify ourselves through obedience to the rules. We sense the need to justify ourselves, and obeying the rules is a way toward that end. I have known lots of Christians who prided themselves in not doing anything really bad. Your obedience never leads to freedom, it leads to deeper disobedience—namely pride. In fact, unbelief in free grace is arrogance because the unbelieving does not find within self a reason to believe God for their salvation.

Remember the story of the prodigal son? Well, the typical church's version often neglects Jesus' opening line: "There was a man who had two sons" (Luke 15:11). It was a parable of two sons, one who rejected the father through his rebellion and selfish consumption, and one son who rejected the father through his enslaving obedience. We are told that the son who stayed was angry and refused to welcome home his younger, repentant brother, and his father's invitation to the party.

Jesus continued, "His father came out and entreated him, but he answered his father, 'Look, these many years I have served you, and

I never disobeyed your command, yet you never gave me a young goat, that I might celebrate with my friends'" (Luke 15:28-29).

Literally it reads, "Never at any time did I neglect a command of Yours" and the rest, though unspoken, is "so I expect my goodness to be rewarded." This is the pride of life, that we put our moral record together, work hard for God, and wrongly believe we put God into our debt. We believe, *I am owed.* Every religion on earth is like this. It is production oriented, hoping God accepts what you and I have done.

This story was aimed as a warning to moral, righteous, good people who were devoted to traditional moral values and take their pride in living by them. Even if they mess up, they still did part of it and God makes up for what they lacked anyway.

Jesus exploded the myths of religious pride, and His audience—both the "sinners" and the "moral" people—was in shock. They had never heard of a God like this. And the arrogant Pharisees, who had "never disobeyed" God's commands, knew He was talking about them.

Want to know if your obedience is motived by pride? Are you envious of others who seem to get God's blessing and you feel you aren't? "It is not fair," you mumble. Do you write people off as beyond hope? "There is no way for him/her to be a Christian." You wrongly think, *I was good enough to get in*, but can't see how that person could ever be saved.

How about comparing yourself to others' sins? *I would never do that. I would never have done such a thing as that,* you think. That is coming from a place of pride in your obedience.

You may also see arrogance by being an unforgiving person. "Shouldn't he have to pay? Isn't there some sort of time they have to serve? Isn't there some level of groveling to be done before we just let them off the hook?" If you grew up with a religion that took pride in their purity and wanted you to do the same, they lied to you.

Open-hearted obedience. Finally, we can obey God with an open heart, or in an unconditioned way, as a grateful response to His grace. My wife, Rachel, has a nephew who went to college and complained that he had to take Spanish in order to graduate. He paid the tuition, hated every class, and barely passed. "I took the class," he said, "but I did not learn Spanish." After college, however, he met a girl from Colombia, South America. He fell in love with her, so he paid a tutor and learned Spanish. The desire to learn her language wasn't because of the "have to have a second language" rule to graduate, but rather because he loved.

When the vitality of grace penetrates the deepest motivations of our hearts, our new direction in life is to make much of Christ not ourselves. We become generous, as it were, in our obedience to follow Him because of love. "If you love me, you will obey my teaching and commands," Jesus reminded His disciples (see John 14:15, 21, 23-24; 15:10; 1 John 5:3) because He first loved us (see John 15:9, 12; 2 John 4:9, 16).

Think about it. What would it look like in your city if everyone treated everyone else exactly the way they were meant to be treated? I know it's hard to imagine, but just dream for a moment about what that might look like if we loved our neighbor as ourselves. In just one year how would your city change? It would be rid of racism and inequality. Rape, murder, theft, and assaults would disappear.

Marriages would strengthen and children would freely play together with wild abandonment. Education would be better and poverty nearly eradicated. Almost back to Eden. Almost like what most of us see as the way things ought to be.

However, we know the law can't make people do those things. The law cannot change our hearts. God didn't tell us to love one another the way we love ourselves because, by doing so, we would clean up our acts and be acceptable to Him. And it definitely wasn't a power play on His part to show He's the boss.

God's intention was not to force us into obedience with rules, but to show us how messed up our lives really are. It was to show what life ought to be like, as we were originally designed to live. And if we follow His revealed ways while living in the land of amazing grace, being influenced by His grace, we become influencers who love, enjoy life with God and others, offer mercy as good "Samaritans," forgive parents, spouses, or friends as we've been forgiven, and persevere in hardship or persecution. Open-hearted obedience operates along with faith and true repentance for Christ's fame and our good. Obedience, then, is a joy-filled response to grace. It really becomes a generous (or unguarded) obedience in the sense that it isn't forced but liberal, in that it comes from faith in Christ as the highest good.

Our struggle throughout all our lives will be with doubting God and His love for us, and that will lead to disobeying God. The world screams at us, our own inner insecurities plague us, and the Evil One whispers it in our ears, *There is no God to rescue you, you are on your own, so make life work for yourself, your way*. It began in the first garden, as we saw in the backstory, so it has been that way for a long time.

The temptation to make life work on our own, to disobey God, reveals how we look to find satisfaction in life. How we resist, temptation reveals how we find satisfaction with Christ. Our obedience is not a way to earn God's approval, it's an open-hearted, grateful response to His love to renew us. Let me restate a principle I made already: the love of God for us is the beauty of the gospel and the motivational pull of the Spirit. Our obedience flows from the freedom of God's vital grace freely given. The quality of gratitude is at the center of a life influenced by vital grace. Why? Because generosity is the core of Christianity. It is the gospel of grace, and it is the mark of a radically changed heart.

Gospel 3D in Living Color

To live in vital grace we need to regularly practice the three dimensions. Distress (repentance, confession of sin), delight (faith in Christ), and direction (unguarded and open-hearted obedience to Christ) are to be the living color of our lives. Sometimes we keep in step with the Spirit's direction by acting in love, even before we "feel" loving. Obeying God, loving our neighbor, is always the right option, whether we are ready to repent or delight in Christ again. Sometimes we sense the distress of not loving God or others and we turn (repent) from our former lives of loving ourselves more than others. Richard Lovelace reminds us that "the entrance and growth of new spiritual life involves the shattering of our sphere of darkness by repentant faith in redemptive truth. If the Fall [the Ruin] occurred through the embracing of lies, the recovery process of salvation must center on faith in truth, reversing the condition."[10]

Sometimes, our step in the Spirit is to first find delight in Christ. As C. S. Lewis says, "Relying on God has to begin all over again every day as if nothing had yet been done."[11] We live "self-controlled" (Titus 2:11) because our affections are realigned to a greater desire, the beauty and greatness of Jesus. God saves us from the evil in us and around us by filling our hearts with something stronger and higher—a greater love—by the expulsive power of a stronger influence, namely Himself. When the desires of our former lives come, we look to a greater desire. We fight to win by fighting at the level of desire because true obedience flows from faith in Christ, the greatest treasure.

It is the apostle Paul who informs us that as we are growing in the land of amazing grace, the Spirit's influence changes us internally and produces an influencing life on others (see Galatians 5:22-23). Having the Holy Spirit's influence and influencing is what it means to be a Christian. One of the key ways we know He is alive in us is seeing our lives connect with others in kind affection and acts of mercy. The joy of His work in us overflows to life around us.

Stop listening to the whisper of your heart that you must work out your own salvation. Instead remind yourself every single day, moment by moment, that because of His mercy-love, Jesus is at work in you by His Spirit. He wants to realign you to His calling and direction. To be clear, distress (confession and repentance) and delight (faith in Christ) don't lead to direction (obedience to Christ) and then you have arrived. Living in 3D is a colorful life of the 3Ds working together until the moment you take your last breath on earth.

As you live in this way, you will discover your life engaging with the lost world around you in new ways. Your job or career will take on a new perspective—you will be working for the Lord, not for money or fame, since you know that you will receive an inheritance from the Lord as a reward. It is the Lord Christ you are serving (see Colossians 3:24-25).

If you are not a follower of Jesus today, repenting, believing, and obeying God is not something you will choose to do. Why? Because it means death to yourself and your self-saving strategies to make life work. You cannot let go of this world and what it offers because it is all you have. Let me explain.

Several years ago, I discovered I had a severe reaction to shrimp. On one occasion, at a friend's backyard party, I unknowingly ate some. It almost killed me. I now know that any shellfish will kill me. If I was famished and you placed before me a plate of liver and onions and a fried shrimp platter, as much as I detest liver and onions, I will never choose shrimp, even though I have the freedom to do so. Why? Because it would kill me. You will never choose a God who invites you to die to self. And that is why vital grace is a gift given by God to you. The Holy Spirit of God must change you. This is why vital grace is getting everything for nothing.

Scottish pastor Thomas Chalmers wisely counseled:

> Salvation by grace, salvation by free grace, salvation not by obedience but according to the mercy of God, is indispensable to . . . godliness. Retain a single shred or fragment of legality with the Gospel, and you take away the power of the Gospel to melt and reconcile. For this purpose, the freer it is, the better it is.

Along with the light of a free Gospel, the love of the Gospel enters. To the measure that you impair Gospel freeness, you also chase away this love. And never does the sinner find within himself so mighty a moral transformation, as when under the belief that he is saved by grace, he feels constrained thereby to offer his heart as a devoted thing to God, and to eschew [abstain or avoid] ungodliness. [12]

You may have been churched most of your life. What would you answer if a gospel mentor got close enough and asked, "What is the present value of grace in your life?" Would you know a good answer? A real answer? Does the grace given to you in Christ offer any real hope of life change?

Here is the thing: You may feel trapped by a lifestyle you hate. You are enslaved to it and have promised you'd never to do that awful behavior again. In a secret place of your heart, you are afraid you're never really going to change.

Or you may feel as though you are dying today. Your insides are crushed by unrealized dreams and the loss is more than you can take. You may wonder, *Will I ever recover? Will I ever feel a sense of smile on my heart?*

Or you may be running away from God today. You might look good on the outside, but your insides are in a distant land. You wonder, *Is there even a need to change?* You may be doubting it is possible to live without being so neurotic. The real question is, "Does vital grace really change me?" I would answer yes because that is the business Christ is in.

Let's return briefly to the story Jesus told about the two sons. Understand that it is a micro-story of God's bigger story of grace. Remember the first two brothers, Cain and Abel, in Genesis 4? One brother went missing (Cain had killed Abel), so God asked Cain, "Where is your brother?" And the famous reply was, "Am I my brother's keeper?" God's implied answer was, "Yes, yes you are your brother's keeper." In Luke 15, Jesus told three stories—the shepherd who looked for the lost sheep, the woman who looked for the lost coin, and then the father with his two sons. But the older son did not look for the younger son.

However, there is another Son who is telling the story. There is a true Brother who loved His lost brothers and sisters that He came to seek and save them. Jesus is the ultimate Hero of the Story. God planned a whole history to be run a certain way so that this Son—the true older Brother—could have all the fame and that His righteousness—not yours, but His—would be the issue before God. The gospel of grace is that Jesus is the sole and only ground of our acceptance with God.

Thousands of men and women have been rescued from worldly despair through this vital grace, and there are Christians whose lives have been saved from the despair of legalism and moralism. He is changing people by grace alone through faith alone in Him alone. Vital grace gives strength to one who has none and blesses those who live by it.

SEVEN

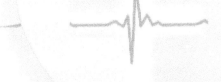

Graced Again and Again and Again...

It is good for our hearts to be strengthened by grace, not by doing religious things.
Hebrews 13:9

Have you ever noticed that once you hear a song and think it says one thing, even when you read the lyric, it is difficult not to sing what you were singing all those times before? When Elton John's song "Tiny Dancer" is on the radio, one of my daughters is still convinced that he says, "Hold me closer, I'm tired of dancing," instead of the correct lyrics, "Hold me closer, tiny dancer." This doesn't just happen with song lyrics. It can happen with Scripture as well.

Throughout most of my life, when I have heard someone quote Jesus' words, "I stand at the door and knock. If anyone hears my voice and opens the door, I will come in and eat with that person, and they with me" (Revelation 3:20), almost exclusively they are using that passage as an evangelistic invitation to "receive Jesus into your heart." You might have only heard it used that way as well so it may be hard to hear it any other way. Because we have misheard it, we've missed Jesus' powerful and instructive invitation of being strengthened by His vital grace. Let me show you.

The context of Jesus' words is from the apostle John's letter to the Christians in Laodicea, which was a sister town to Colossae just to its north (the book of Colossians was written for the church there). In his letter, Paul told the pastor at Colossae to read their letter (the book of Colossians) to the Laodicean church (see Colossians 4:16) and for them to read the letter he had sent to Laodicea (though we do not have that letter in the Bible).

John's letter to Laodicea (and the other six churches in Revelation 2 and 3) was written about thirty-five years after Paul's letter. This message was Christ's warning to most of the members in the church about their self-reliant complacency in their riches and goodness. He called them back to living by grace alone.

Jesus pointed out in Revelation 3:15 that they were not hot (*zestos*, literally boiling hot) or cold (*psychros*, literally cold). He was saying in effect, "Your lives are not refreshing at all, one way or the other. You are neither a great double-shot expresso or an island smoothie of fruit and ice. You are lukewarm. Who wants to sit down with a good friend and drink lukewarm coffee?" We would agree to a mid-morning spot of hot tea or coffee with a British friend for, as they say, an "Elevenses" or an iced tea after yard work, but room temperature tea is not refreshing after a sweaty day of yard work. Jesus was saying, "You are not refreshing." Why?

They said, "We have grown our wealth and are now very rich." The city was famous for its millionaires and many of the members were probably wealthy business owners in banking, farming, medicine, and textiles. Of course, there is nothing wrong with being successful in business, growing income, generating wealth, and being prosperous. The woman praised in Proverbs 31 was a profitable business owner who was industrious ("She considers a field and buys it; out of her earnings she plants a vineyard. She sets about her work vigorously: she sees that her trading is profitable"), thrifty ("She makes linen garments and sells them; she provides food for her family and portions for her female workers"), and generous with what she earned ("She opens her arms to the poor and extends her hands to the needy").

However, Jesus goes to the heart of their problem. They said, because of their wealth, "We have need of nothing." The former life, seen in the city's cultural idolatry, still dominated over their new lives. They had accepted Jesus, but they relied on their wealth (their surface idol) for their status and their personal and family security, along with the comforts wealth could provide (their source idols).

Jesus' strong words remind us of what a loving Father does; namely, He called them back to reality: "You are wretched, pitiful, poor, blind, and naked" (Revelation 3:17). If a friend said to you, "Your zipper is down" or "You have a stain on the back of your shirt" would you take that as judging you? I highly doubt it. Jesus' words to His sons and daughters may sound condemning to our sensibilities, but it's not. If we reasoned from the lesser to the greater, a stain on a shirt or a stained heart, it really would be quite loving to point out the stained heart. Love would not want a friend, much less sons and daughters, to remain in a pitiful, poor, and wretched condition.

He continued, "Those I love I discipline." The writers of Proverbs and Hebrews echoed, just as a father disciplines his loved children so the Lord disciplines the ones He loves (Proverbs 3:12, Hebrews 12:5). Plainly, Jesus was speaking to His children, whom He loves.

Vital grace, unlike the core of other religions, is centered in and on God's mercy-love. Take His love out of the equation, which as we saw is exactly what our Enemy has done since his evil whisper in the first garden, and we are left with a harsh tyrannical dictator or cruel dad who is concerned only with our unquestioned fealty and loyalty to the rules given.

Then what happened? Jesus invited them to a renewed faith, a reminder to come back to Him: "I counsel you, buy from me gold refined in the fire, so you can become rich; and white clothes to wear, so you can cover your shameful nakedness; and salve to put on your eyes, so you can see" (Revelation 3:18). He offered a clear reference to another time when men and women were invited to "come and buy, without money and without cost. . . . Come to me that your soul may live" (Isaiah 55).

"Hear me," Jesus said, "You need the real, lasting wealth only I can give. You need to live in my righteousness so you are not shamed and have the eyes of your inner being enlightened so you can see what is unseen, because we walk by faith not by sight."

He also called them to confession of their sin and repentance: "Be earnest" (completely intent or literally, *bubble over because you are boiling hot*) to turn from your false belief that you have need of nothing. "It is pitiful" or as the saying goes, "The emperor has no clothes."

Then comes the famous verse: "Here I am! I stand at the door and knock. If anyone hears my voice and opens the door, I will come in and eat with that person, and they with me" (Revelation 3:20).

Living by grace opens the door to fellowship with Christ. The Bible uses many different words for this reality. We are to *dwell, abide, remain, yield, walk, eat, partake*, and other similar concepts that are word pictures of this principle that if we are going to "dine with Christ," we are going to have to be "in Him" by His grace, no longer relying on our former way of life, and we are going to have to keep dining with Him moment by moment.

In John 14:21-23, Jesus made a stunning invitation to His followers. No other god of any religion would say something like it: "Anyone who loves me will obey my teaching. My Father will love them, and *we will come to them and make our home with them*" (emphasis added). A few minutes later Jesus continued, "Remain in me, as I also remain in you. No branch can bear fruit by itself; it must remain in the vine. Neither can you bear fruit unless you remain in me" (John 15:4-5).

Jesus invites you and me to allow the transcendent, personal, all-glorious God to be totally engaged in our lives, as a regular and normative lifestyle. Not figuratively, but literally, to make the real you a place where He lives. No other religion offers such a thing.

My deepest awareness of myself is that I am deeply loved by Jesus Christ, and I have done nothing to earn it or deserve it. We have been granted access to grace through many different channels. As we discipline ourselves to them, we are growing in grace because they are ways we continue to dine with Christ, to have Him, as it were, enter in and eat with us. They will enlarge our capacity to hear God speak and, as a result, to generate inner force that will guide and empower our minds and outer lives.

But what is the metaphor of the door? What is Jesus knocking on? Is it your heart? Is it the door of the church? What should be clear is that Jesus is not pleading with a non-believer to open the door of his or her heart and let him in. He is talking to a congregation of Christians.

Often in the Bible, the door is used as a figure of speech for judgment. The idea first appears when God warned Cain about his murderous heart ("a sin sacrifice is laying at the door" in Genesis 4:7). Jesus used the doors and doorkeeper to indicate His return as Judge in Mark 13:32-37.

Back to Jesus' word to individuals in the church of Laodicea. While the opportunity to eat with Christ is offered, there is an alternative implied by "at the door": *judgment.*

Jesus said that He was the only door by which we can enter His kingdom. Jesus taught, "I am the door, and you must enter by the door" (John 10:7). If you enter through Christ's door, you can go in and go out, and you will find pasture (eating). Jesus added, "I have come to give a full life." This leads to fellowship with Christ, as His people know His voice and follow it.

So here is a door of dividing—some are in and some out of the flock, but He is the door. He is the "door of hope" (Hosea 2:15). He not only judges but He is the judged. The judgment and the judged. We must never extract the Lover from His judgment because He took all the judgment needed, giving us everything we need.

Jesus is not begging or powerlessly pleading with you to open the door. If you are in Him, you will hear His voice and He will come in and create the deepest friendship possible. The closest friendship of a father with a daughter or son. It is about remaining in each other: "remain in me and I will remain in you" (verse 4). Another translation uses the word *abide*.

You and I have the possibility of every moment being connected to God and having Him bring out all that is wonderful in and through us. Our calling is to have an active passivity. We remain, but His life is pulsating into us. This is how we grow grace in our lives.

How Do We Know that We Are Dining with Christ?

The question is often, how do we know when we are dining (or abiding) in Christ? The answer: when we want others, by sheer delight, to know the love we know; to experience the beauty and wonder of grace we have experienced. We are dining with Christ when His love for us has moved us from pride to humility as we recognize his truly amazing, vital grace at work in our lives.

We reach out to others who are poor because we were poor. We reach out to our neighbors because Jesus came and moved in as our neighbor. We forgive because we know forgiveness. We are generous with our worldly wealth as a response to His generosity.

If you live with a nagging fear over God's power and justice and not in the joy of His goodness, you probably are not growing in grace. If you fear God as Judge who is seeking cause to imprison you and do not see Him as your Friend and Father, you are probably not growing in grace. When your sense of hope in the gospel is tied to how well you are doing with Christian duties, you are not growing in grace. If you believe God's promise of eternal life is based on Jesus *along with* something you provide, you are not growing in God's grace.

As I mentioned before, I was a Christian for more than a decade before I knew any other way of salvation than to ask for forgiveness and strive with all my effort to live a good and obedient life, the way my teachers and preachers told me, in order to keep up my friendship with God. I was a good kid, but a well-behaved (on the outside), proud and judgmental Pharisee. I had "invited Jesus into my heart" but had also accepted a responsibility to engage my will and effort to restrain my desires for my self-absorbed life. I did not rely on my personal wealth, I had none. Nevertheless, I relied on my spiritual bank account through my moral behavior. I could not believe He was fond of me and wanted to hang out and eat with me, much less throw a party for me (see Luke 15:23-24).

When our freedom is tied to how well we are doing with Christian duties, we will only feel free to the degree we are either doing what we think is our duty or by casting off any sense of duty at all. I lived long and hard on the duty side of that equation.

This is important to remember when we begin to seriously ask ourselves, "Does grace, in any ongoing way, continue to strengthen us day by day?" Are there any rules to live by? Is it, as one pastor said, "Love God and live holy" or is it reducible to "Love God and do whatever you want?" If there is a way in which grace can be strengthened in life, what is it?

Is There a Way to Strengthen Grace in Our Lives?

In some church traditions, the way we are strengthened is through what we call the "means of grace." It always seemed, though, to be more about the "means" than the grace. Are the "means" by which grace is strengthened in a life the same as living by a new set of rules? Church teaching on Christian living by grace can be confusing, I know, and I have "mastered the divine" (I received a master of divinity and a doctorate as well). If it's confusing to me, I can only imagine what it is for people sitting in church a couple Sundays a month who get conflicting messages. "God has done His part, now you do your part" seems to be at least what is implied.

Our recurring theme has been that vital grace is God giving you everything for nothing. The true story began with the Good News that we were made in the image of the King of creation to be His managers over all He made and to find joy and life in Him. But as we have also seen, we need grace because our earthly lives were and continue to be ruined by our self-oriented choices. We "sold ourselves" into a slavery of our inordinate and uncontrolled desires (see John 8:34; Romans 7:14). We are under a curse of death and no matter how much we try to avoid it, work around it, or chase other heroes to rescue us, we remain helpless and spiritually dead. That is the bad news.

However, we have very good news. Jesus Christ rescued us by paying the price to buy us back, removing the curse, and freeing us from our enslavement. When we stop believing that we can rescue ourselves—that is, we quit relying on our efforts or non-efforts (repentance)—and start relying (faith) in His life, death, and resurrection as ours by free grace alone, then we are translated into an eternal connection with Christ, made complete in Him, dead to the old self, alive to God, and given His Spirit with an implanted new desire to love and follow the "One who loved me and gave himself for me" (generous obedience). If this reality is not present in a person's life, it probably means that the new life was not implanted, no matter if he or she says they "invited Jesus into their heart."

Millions of people throughout history have had God miraculously alter their lives. Those men and women showed us the paths to follow once transformed by grace. Just as the writer to Hebrews encouraged his readers that it is "good for our hearts to be strengthened by grace" (13:9), and Paul exhorted Timothy to "be strengthened by the grace that is in Christ Jesus" (2 Timothy 2:1), I want to encourage you to be strengthened by grace in your journey by increasing the truth and reality of vital grace's influence in deepening your love for Christ. The path of true spirituality is the path our first parents were designed to walk on and that, as we have seen, they chose to leave. The way back is by God's grace alone. And God has graciously implanted into us His Spirit to press grace down into the operational systems of our hearts, so we continue to live healthy in His grace.

Granted, some people have turned the ways He works into new rules or laws to follow. But let's not make a counter-mistake and end up refusing Christ's invitation to dine with Him (remember we got everything) just so we don't become moralists or rule keepers. Without using the ways God has granted us, we put ourselves in the high-risk category. Our spiritual immune system against the enemies of grace (namely the Evil One, the world's pressured consensus, the false teachers in our churches, and our own remaining temptation to rely on ourselves) will be compromised just as it was for the Christians in Laodicea.

I noted at the start that we too easily forget God's grace and it leaks out of us. We must continually remind ourselves and one another of what is true Truth. As I have told the multiple dozens of brides and grooms on their wedding day, "Love has to be nurtured and tended. There are no guarantees that the love you feel today will be there three, five, or ten years from now."

The love you have from God and the love you had for God when you began the new life will not automatically or naturally remain alive in your heart and mind. You must feed it to grow. Loving God does not come naturally, loving self does. Love for Christ is supernatural and one of the ways it remains is to remember His love.

Let's explore the ordinary ways God has given to us that provide us with the joy of being strengthened by His grace alone. These ways are present in a normal Christian life (nothing magical in them, but they are supernatural by the Holy Spirit) as we interact and connect with God at the deepest level (metaphor for "dine with him") and we "taste and see that the LORD is good" (Psalm 34:8).

We Dine with Him through the Bible

It is reasonable to believe that if an infinite loving God exists, He would desire to communicate Himself to the ones He made, even if they had committed rebellion. And it is also a reasonable assumption that being a personal Creator, He would use both words and actions in the very lives or in the moment of history in which they lived to communicate to them. And it is completely reasonable that He would have His creatures use language to record His communication since He would want to continue His communication through time.

One of the unique characteristics about humanness is our ability to read and write! He would not have to write things that only a supranatural being would know, He would only have to reveal Himself in ways that were human so we could know Him.

He did and it is called the Bible. It is not the purpose of this book to prove that the Bible is the direct revelation from God, but plenty of resources and experts can help you with that. The Bible is where we learn of the need for grace, and we are stimulated to grow in that grace when we read the Bible. Reading the Bible is essential to life in vital grace.

Ann Voskamp dramatically captures the power of reading the Bible in *One Thousand Gifts:*

> I open a Bible, and His plans, startling, lie there barefaced. It's hard to believe it, when I read it, and I have to come back to it many times . . . [to] make sure [the words] are real. His love letter forever silences any doubts: "His secret purpose from the very beginning [is] to bring us to our full glory" (1 Corinthians 2:7 NEB). He means to rename us—to return us to our true names, our truest selves. . . . From the very beginning, that Eden beginning, that has always been and always is, to this day, His secret purpose—our return to *our full glory.*[1]

Psalms are filled with reminders of how powerful God's revelation to us, through His Word, clarifies, cleanses, and corrects our paths for our highest good. Eugene Peterson writes in *The Message,* his interpretation of Psalm 119:1-5, 9-12:

You're blessed when you stay on course, walking steadily on the road revealed by GOD. You're blessed when you follow His directions, doing your best to find him. That's right—you don't go off on your own; you walk straight along the road he set. You, GOD, prescribed the right way to live. How can a person live a clean life? By carefully reading the map of your Word. I'm single-minded in pursuit of you; don't let me miss the road signs you've posted. I've banked your promises in the vault of my heart, so I won't sin myself bankrupt. Be blessed, GOD; train me in your ways of wise living.

If you want to know God's love and presence and have grace grab you, you must read the Bible as God's amazing rescue story of grace to those who have been ruined. As Albert Wolters wrote:

To miss the grand narrative of Scripture is a serious matter; it is not simply a matter of misinterpreting parts of Scripture. It is a matter of being oblivious to which story is shaping our lives. When the Bible is broken up into little bits and chunks— theological, devotional, spiritual, moral, or world-view bits and chunks—then these bits can be nicely fitted into the reigning story of our own culture with all its idols! The Bible loses is forceful and formative power by being absorbed into a more encompassing secular story.[2]

Having a printed Bible you can read, underline, take notes, study, and memorize is most advantageous to getting the power of the gospel of grace deep in your inner thought life. One method some have found helpful is to read and make observations on what the passage teaches or reveals about God or Christ (Who is God? What Christ has done for me?). Then ask what it says about you (Who am I? What is the best way for me to live in grace as a daughter or son?).

Most everyone carries with them the ability to have a Bible to read or be read to them because almost everyone has a smart phone. I encourage you to download either *YouVersion* or *The Public Reading of Scripture* apps and engage in the Bible as regular rhythms of life.

When we read the Bible, we are listening to His voice and He is "dining" with us, as it were. God's vital grace is Christ. Grace is not a commodity or something we apply, like skin cream or "sin cream." Grace is Christ being everything we need for us, and His story is a love story that shapes His grace into love! Reading the Bible is one way we get grace down into our lives by dining with Him in His Word.

We Dine with Him through Prayer

Not every believer of Christianity has had the privilege of reading the Bible. Even today, in many countries, owning a Bible is illegal. When it was being penned over the six thousand years of history, the average person was not literate, nor did they have anything to read. However, there is one deep expression every Christ follower does have to enrich grace in life, and that is immediate access to God in prayer. In Christ, we have instant access to God: "Let us approach the throne of grace with confidence, so that we may receive mercy and find grace to help us in our time of need" (Hebrews 4:16). Prayer is an invitation to friendship with God, it is not simply a religious activity we are to do. As we pray to God, we *find grace to help us!*

I understand that most of us feel ashamed of our prayer life—or I should say our lack of prayer life. Many people I have mentored or coached along the way have freely shared the lack of consistency in praying to God in any meaningful way. "I pray in my car on the way to work" or "I pray in the shower" are two common places of prayer I hear about most often. But this is to see prayer through a religious lens or activity and not one that has been pushed down into the soul because of vital grace. Don't get me wrong, I am glad people pray in their cars. I think seven out of ten Americans say they pray every week.[3] We don't know what people actually mean by prayer, but that statistic has remained fairly steady for decades.

When we see prayer as being in friendship related to the reality that God has given everything we need as a free gift, it will become mostly a conversation in gratitude, worship, confession, and enjoyment with a loving and kind Father. When it isn't, prayer becomes mostly a shopping list of more things for God to do or cries for relief out of some trouble or discomfort. Prayer like that is a transactional relationship with Christ and not with a person we are dining with.

The spiritual gift of prayer is given to some people, and my wife is one of them. She prays about things I never consider. She talks to God, and God enriches her faith and dispenses a grace that keeps her loving, serving, and caring for others, including a dependent, special-needs adult. One thing I have learned seeing her pray every morning for more than forty-three years is that the vital grace of God not only *has* power for her life, but *is* also power, and it meets her in prayer.

Jesus' disciples had learned rote prayers from their parents. Every Jewish child did. There is nothing wrong with that. In fact, using the prayers from the ancients is a good way to learn how to pray. The disciples often saw Jesus pray and one day they said, "Lord, teach us to pray." So He gave them a model or an outline to follow through the Lord's Prayer (see Luke 11:1-13). Growing up, we recited the Lord's Prayer in our weekly worship service. The model was to show us the how. My close friend John Smed wrote, "[Jesus] has given us a simple but comprehensive outline for prayer that is filled with promise and purpose. This prayer is a summary of what God's kingdom is all about. . . . Because this is a prayer Jesus gave, it cannot fail to be heard and answered."[4]

Once Jesus gave them the "how" to pray, He told them a story to show them the "why" of prayer. He used a story of Matt who went to his friend Nate's house in middle of the night and asked if he could have some bread for a guest who just arrived. Matt told him to quietly go away. But Nate kept knocking, and Matt finally got up and gave him some bread. (Okay, Jesus did not use names.)

We must understand this parable is not a story of comparison where Jesus is suggesting, "If you pray enough and be persistent enough like Matt was with Nate, you will wear God down and He will finally get up and meet your need." Instead, Jesus was using it as a contrast. Jesus concluded His story to show us why can we approach the throne of grace with confidence:

I say to you: Ask and it will be given to you; seek and you will find; knock and the door will be opened to you. If you then, though you are evil, know how to give good gifts to your friends, how much more will your Father in heaven give the Holy Spirit to those who ask! (Luke 11:9-13)

He showed us that we have a true Friend, who is more than willing to do much more than we can even ask or imagine. He can be approached and is never annoyed. He is for us and wants to answer our needs—to provide His daily bread. His Kingdom has and will come. He will give us the Holy Spirit and the power to believe vital grace is true—that He really has given us everything as we "dwell, eat, dine, abide" by prayer conversations with Him. God meets us at the intersection of our prayer life because it connects us with Him, His kingdom, and His mission, and knowing Him and joining Him on His mission is the greatest life any of us can attain.

Prayer is both the give and take in our friendship with God and is a major way for us to be strengthened by grace. It is the greater work of God. We do not have to have an education, be a pastor, or be a master-level religious person to connect to God in prayer.

Our prayerlessness really isn't about a lack of knowing how to pray but is a direct result of our core desire to rely mostly on our own ability, wealth, and wisdom. We must increase our affection for Christ by talking to God with intentionality and with regularity. Kingdom prayer is a prayer life that engages and activates faith, repentance, and our desire to follow hard after God. Kingdom prayer enlarges our eyes and faith. It is a way we "fix our eyes" on Jesus, as Originator (the author or one who takes the lead) and Finisher (the one who completes) of grace in our lives. I invite you to contact the folks at Prayer Current (www.prayercurrent.com) or *A Praying Life* (www.seejesus.net/training/welcome-praying-life) and use the materials to increase your Kingdom-centered prayer capacity both personally and with others in your church community.

We Dine with Him through Church

Church has been a cultural activity in many parts of the United States for a long time. However, going to church in our Western culture is losing its appeal. Most of the church gurus have data to show how church attendance is waning. I get it. It can be difficult to attend church sometimes.

There is coming a time, maybe it has already found us, that being part of a church will be countercultural, the way it was in the early days of Acts. However, when the early first-century Christians began to identify their lives with Christ, they also identified their lives with one another. New churches sprung up all over the known world and, due to the lack of large spaces and persecution, they met primarily in homes. The historian Luke described what they did as they connected their lives in their new identities: they "devoted" themselves to worship, the Lord's supper, teaching, loving one another, offering mercy, prayer meetings, living generously, and disciple-making (see Acts 2:42-47).

As new churches were started in cities and communities, they identified themselves to one another so deeply that Paul instructed them that if someone in their church who had claimed to be a

Christian was living like a pagan non-Christian, they should be "put out of your fellowship" (1 Corinthians 5:2). As a countercultural community, they had an identity to Christ and to one another. They were turning away from the cultural, city, and family idols and quickly discovered that being part of a church community was a way to get grace pushed down into their new way of life. There are many important factors of being in a church to enlarge our grace capacity:

We gather to worship God. Our first parents were made to worship God in their "community." Their ruin, by being captivated by something besides their Maker, destroyed not only their capacity for relationship but their community with God. As we saw in the backstory, that decision not only affected them but their immediate children, all the way to the counterfeit worshiping people who built their worship center in Babel (see Genesis 11).

Worshiping God with other Christ followers is part of our original design. The worship leader, Asaph, confessed his struggle to believe God is good and loving when he saw how the morally corrupt people around him seemed to have such prosperous and easy lives. He readily admitted that he almost slipped away, thinking it was a mistake to keep on being faithful to God until he "entered the sanctuary of God," then he remembered, "Who do I have in life but God" (Psalm 73). Worshiping God with others who loved and worshiped God refreshed grace in life.

Yes, worship is to be a way of life, but grace is in some mysterious way enlarged in our inner cores when we sing, pray, confess, and remind ourselves of our lives with God with others who are singing, praying, and confessing. If we are not captivated by God's beauty (His holiness) nor offended by our own ugliness, we will become enamored by our own beauty (our goodness, good works, sincerity, well intentions) and offended by God's presumed "ugliness" (ruling, kingship, authority to judge). Entering the sanctuary in worship of God reorients our hearts to what is the best.

We gather to hear accurate gospel teaching. We grow in grace by hearing Christ-exalted, grace-centered preaching and teaching. Our souls need to hear God's Word explained accurately by those who have studied and prepared. But not just any teaching; it must be teaching of God's unearned grace. There are plenty of moralistic preachers offering pep talks or pronouncements on us staying holy, and probably more who deliver captivating, inspirational messages, making us the heroes of our stories, while cheering us on with words like *believe* and *faith*. In the end, they both weaken the vitality of grace in our lives. What will strengthen us is to be taught and retaught the grace of God through Christ, who has done it all.

We gather to experience authentic community. The author of Hebrews warns us not to neglect assembling together (see 10:25). It is a hostile world, and we need other believers because we need encouragement in the faith. We are battered all day long with conflicting messages about life, meaning, and sources of fulfillment. We constantly wrestle with doubts of God's love and the urges of our former lives. When I hear someone articulate their own Emmaus Road experience on how their doubts or struggle was met by a living Jesus, I am re-motivated to remain and dine with Him.

The enemy of God and God's people is constantly on the hunt, to tempt us to disbelieve and "go back to Egypt" (the former life we had). Being with other followers increases grace and faith. Being friends with other Christians is so we continue to know and live in our friendship with God.

A pastor friend and I were sitting by a nighttime fire in his backyard. I had been his guest at a leadership retreat and we were unplugging from the weekend. At the time he was the leading a solid, missionally engaged church that was doing significant things in his city. We began to talk seriously about pastor friends who had blown themselves up, who had abandoned the ministry, their call, and sometimes their family. Most had been faithful, godly pastors, caring for a church and many for a long time. Then *wham*! They tanked. They quit. They were fired. They threw their lives into the shredder.

My friend and I confessed our own independence. We are basically loners. Ministry can have that effect on people (or is it loners are attracted to ministry?). We repented to God and each other. It was authentic community. We encouraged each other with gospel truths about who God is and who we were as men and told stories of what God had done and was doing. That is what Christian community is for grace-oriented lives.

We gather to celebrate the Lord's Supper and baptism. We must also realize that part of church life involves baptism and celebrating the Lord's Supper or Communion together. We proclaim Christ's life and death on our behalf when we take Communion, and we are remembered back into Him. Is there a more tangible way that describes us dining, remaining in Jesus, than acting out the eating and drinking of His death and resurrection in Communion?

And water baptism signifies and reminds us that it is by grace, not our effort and works, as well as seals us into Him (Rom 6:3-4).

As Augustine said, they are "visible signs of invisible grace."[5] In other words, they point to the real thing—Jesus Christ.

We Dine with Him through Music

I happen to believe that the older men and women who told us that the means of grace were only the Word, the sacraments, prayer, and the church would have included music if they'd had access to iTunes or streaming music back then. I think iTunes is the greatest invention known to man since the printing press. Every morning when I wake up, I have a song playing in my head. It's different every day. Sometimes it's a Steven Curtis Chapman tune, sometimes a hymn or a '70s oldie, but there is a song. I stream songs all day long. Music is a window into my soul, so I fill a lot of it with lyrics that remind me of the truth about the gospel, grace, and Jesus' love.

Why? Because there is a whisper in the universe that was put there in the garden that God is not for you, make life work for yourself. Martin Luther said, "To doubt the good will of God is an inborn suspicion of God with all of us."[6]

For me, one of the means of remembering God has not abandoned me is through music. Worship music is a way God's grace is worked down into my operating life. I do not listen to Christian tunes or worship music because I am such a good Christian, but because I am a weak Christian and the worship of God in music reminds and renews grace in my heart. For the sake of your soul, listen and worship God in song. Plug in, go for a walk, and listen to some good tunes.

We Dine with God through
Practicing Regular Generosity

One spiritual reality that we need to consider is this, where you store your wealth is where the center of your life is going to concentrate. Another way grace is awakened and enlivened is by giving away portions of your wealth so your heart does not get fixed on material wealth. Jesus Himself warned that we cannot love both God and money because no one can serve (live for) two masters. You can only love one or the other (Matthew 6:24). When you give it to the Lord, your heart is connected in deeper abiding with Him. "See that you excel in this grace of giving," Paul wrote to the Christians in Corinth (2 Corinthians 8:7) because he wanted to test the sincerity of their love.

When some early wealthy Christians in Jerusalem were captivated by the grace of Christ for them through His death and resurrection, they moved from the 10 percent-tithe rule to being generous, selling personal and family assets so they could give above their tithe to the Lord and have it distributed to others. Luke tells us in Acts 2:45, "They were selling their possessions and belongings [literally converting their acquired wealth of property, land, or portions of their estate] and distributing the money to those who had need." They knew they were responsible to God for their generation and to do so, they needed to be generous with their material wealth.

The practice of generosity deepens our faith. Why? Well, generosity is a quality of a life radically influenced by Christ's grace in giving to us. We believe Jesus when He said, "It is more blessed to give than to receive" (Acts 20:35) because He gave us everything.

Jesus spent His ultimate wealth, the truest treasure in the universe, Himself, for us. God was totally generous in sending His Son, who willingly became poor, even to point of death, so that we could become rich, by loving God the way we need to, covering the shame we bear in life, and paying off the debt we had with the Father.

One thing I do understand about God's kingdom ventures is that, at the very least, our generation is responsible to reach our generation and care for it with the Good News of Jesus Christ, His gracious saving life and acts of mercy and justice. Yes, we have responsibility to leave some inheritance for our children and grandchildren—I know the Bible. But we live here and now and are called to this time, place, and people. Thus generosity needs to be part of our lifestyles.

One of the goals of the Christian ought to be to treasure what God treasures. What does He treasure? Without question, the short answer is that He treasures His own glory in all things. As we have been reminded several times, we are the only creatures in the universe who are the imago Dei (the image of God), and He is glorified in us.

Jesus was asked one day, "Is it right to pay taxes?" He took a coin and replied, "Whose image is on the coin?" Caesar's image was the obvious answer. He then said, "Give to Caesar what is Caesar's, but render to God what is God's." The coin had a pagan's image, so Jesus instructed them to give money, taxes, and earthly stuff to their earthly rulers. However, we are God's image. We are a display of His glory. We are to give to God, us. All of us.

No, we don't have a deal with a God who only asks for 10 percent and we get to do what we want with 90 percent. As we saw earlier, that may have been the attitude of the churched people in Laodicea.

But we are 100 percent His and we are to use our money to treasure other image bearers. That is what love is.

What motivates us to be generous? Christ left the most prestigious and richest gated community in the universe and became poor for you and me, so that we could become rich. He really did give us everything: "For you know the grace of our Lord Jesus Christ, though he was rich, yet for your sakes he became poor, so that you through his poverty might become rich" (2 Corinthians 8:9). He valued you and me and gave all, namely Himself.

When that truth grabs hold of you, or to the degree it does, you won't be able to park your money for years on end giving bits and pieces from the interest earned. When grace is operating in life, you will be diligent to generously distribute your money for the things God treasures.

We Dine with God through Suffering

During a difficult time you may have had a well-meaning friend say to you, "God never gives you more than you can handle." They were, I am sure, trying to help ease the pain. However, it simply is not true. God routinely gives us more than we can handle.

To the members of the church in Corinth, Paul confessed, "We do not want you to be uninformed . . . about the hardships we suffered in . . . Asia. We were under great pressure, far beyond our ability to endure, so that we despaired even of life. Indeed, in our hearts we felt the sentence of death" (2 Corinthians 1:8). Paul despaired even of life, like a death sentence in his heart. That is a great deal of suffering.

Pain and suffering, though universal and inevitable, is one of God's power tools to teach us that His grace really is perfected in our weakness. Suffering and weakness destroy the silly and sad illusion that we have control in this life, but it also increases our faith that God's love is very real and very present in our weakness. Paul concluded his thought on his suffering to the congregation, "[All that suffering and pain] happened that we might not rely on ourselves but on God, who raises the dead." Grace was given. Jesus not only felt the sentence of death, He actually died, and God raised Him from the dead. Our faith is in Christ, and to grow in grace, we need laughter and we need the lament of pain—sometimes physical, sometimes soulish.

Obviously, suffering is not something we choose to do but rather something we experience. Suffering is a way we get grace into life. When we do get more than we can handle "we rejoice in our sufferings, because we know that suffering produces perseverance, perseverance, character and character, hope. And hope does not disappoint us, because *God has poured out his love* into our hearts by the Holy Spirit, who he has given us" (Romans 5:3-5, emphasis added).

J. I. Packer wisely counseled, "God uses chronic pain and weakness, along with other afflictions, as his chisel for sculpting our lives. Felt weakness deepens dependence for Christ for strength each day. The weaker we feel the harder we lean. And the harder we lean the stronger we grow spiritually, even while our bodies waste away. To live with your 'thorn' uncomplainingly—that is, sweet, patient, and free in heart to love and help others, even though every day you feel weak—is true sanctification. It is true healing for the spirit. It is a supreme victory of grace."[7]

For all the effort during the early part of my Christian upbringing to find the one path that would lead to a non-struggling journey, what I discovered is that there is no one-trick pony to ride to arrive at the place where we no longer need grace. We need to be graced again, and then again, and then again, and daily again. And the ways God has chosen for us to receive ongoing grace is through these various paths. There is no one method. All of them are important to deepen our dwelling, dining, or fellowshiping with our Savior, Jesus Christ.

As you delight more and more in His presence you will enjoy more and more of the delight He has for you. You will hear His songs of joy and love for you. And "this is how we know what love is: Jesus Christ laid down His life for us. . . . This is how God showed His love among us: He sent His one and only Son into the world that we might live through Him. . . . And so we know and rely on the love God has for us" (1 John 3:16; 4:9, 16).

This is why knowing and relying on grace is vital to our enjoying a full and free life. Everything we need to enjoy life with God and others has been graciously provided for us in the person of Jesus Christ.

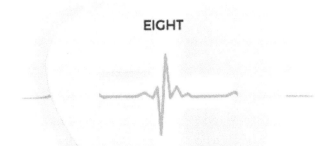

EIGHT

From Influenced to Influencing

God's generous and welcoming heart is to be the hallmark and benchmark of all our
relationships, for it is through our relationships that we represent God to the world.
Scotty Smith, *The Reign of Grace*

A virtually lifeless body of water sits between the countries of Jordan and Israel. It is at the lowest point on earth and its saltiness is some ten times saltier than the ocean, making it impossible for fish or other creatures, besides rare forms of bacteria and algae, to live in it. What makes this sea, known as the Sea of Salt or Dead Sea, so potent an agent of death to life is that water only flows in by rain and from the Jordan River, but it does not flow out. As a result the salt has collected in the sea and has not been a resource for vegetation or animal life. The Dead Sea serves as a metaphor for the life of vital grace.

When we hold onto a form of grace that remains primarily internal or simply as a means to become free from our personal guilt or shame, that grace becomes limited and begins influencing us like a river flowing one way into our lives, as it were. When this happens, we do not experience God's intended purpose for us—or for grace. We haven't made grace vital (essential). Vital grace is about getting everything for nothing, but it doesn't stop there. That vital grace must also lead to us giving grace to others for nothing.

We are influenced by God's Spirit through His grace given to us by Christ's sacrifice on the cross, His resurrection from the dead, and His ascension to His throne. In turn, we become influencers by fulfilling the creation or cultural mandate to exercise dominion over creation, multiply, care for the earth and all in it, and love our neighbor as ourselves (see Genesis 1:28; 2:15; Leviticus 19:18).

Perhaps one reason many leave churches that have good music, teaching, coffee, and kids' programs is because the influence they were receiving never flowed through them into the lives of others in their spheres of influence. They became a dead sea.

During our time together in these pages, we have spent a lot of time making much of the *hesed* love of Christ in His gospel of grace. God's counter-conditional love really is, as mentioned before, the beauty of the gospel and the motivational pull of the Spirit that frees us. It is very good news, and the freer it is the better it is, not the other way around. To the degree we hold onto any form of performance or self-effort, we lessen grace's power to make the transformations God intends. The vitality of grace bursts into a myriad array of wonder and miracles when we are "working together with him" (Christ) in our generation for salvation, because "now is the favorable time" (2 Corinthians 6:1-2, ESV).

If you remember in the backstory, we saw that not only our first parents ruined their lives, we also observed the nations and entire universe as a whole became a runaway. The ruin is cosmic in scope. Christopher Wright insightfully reminds us:

> God's mission is what spans the gap between the curse on the earth of Genesis 3 and the end of the curse in the new creation of Revelation 22. God's mission is what brings humanity from being a cacophony of nations divided and scattered in the rebellion against God in Genesis 11 to being a choir of nations united and gathered in the worship of God in Revelation 7.[1]

God has a mission to reconcile to Himself men and women from all nations who were ruined by the rebellion and He has a people for His mission. We who have been pulled, drawn in, by the Spirit of Christ are also on God's mission to those unreconciled with God, their Creator.

We saw in Chapter Three that God's covenant with Abraham was to offer His grace to the Gentile nations. The grace given to Abraham was to be a "blessing to the nations" (Genesis 12:2-3). Through Abraham, God launched the greatest buy-back program in the universe. He sent His one and only Son to redeem (purchase or buy back) a people as His very own possession, that we would declare to our generation the "excellencies of him who called you out of darkness into his marvelous light" (1 Peter 2:9, ESV). Jesus Christ is the light for the nations and offers His salvation to the ends of the earth. Because God's rescue involved the nations, it is a global gospel and we are carriers of the grace to the world. A cosmic transfer of wealth!

Paul said telling other people of Christ's excellencies was the ministry God had given him and his band of disciples and mentorees. God's message through them was a "ministry of reconciliation" (2 Corinthians 5:18), imploring enemies of God to turn to Him and let God make peace with them.

God's method of caring for His people is His people. And God's plan for reconciling men, women, university students, teenagers, boys, and girls to Himself is by His people. That means when we receive and live by vital grace, God desires us to share that grace with others, leading them not to a program, code of ethics, or societal evolution, but always back to His love and grace.

Gospel Influenced and Influencing Life

The gospel of grace is for nonbelievers but also for believers who are to live by faith (see Romans 1:17). You are to be someone who represents God's reconciling power of the vitality of grace with fellow followers of Jesus as well as those who are not yet followers. Those who now have a new identity in Christ continually need vital grace, and Christ has granted us His Spirit, producing in us who we were designed to be as well as the skills to multiply the gospel of grace in our spheres of influence.

When I ask Christians, "What is the fruit of the Spirit?" those who have read the Bible usually list what the fruit is: "Oh, it's love, joy, and peace," they respond. But they do not explain what fruit means. Fruit is something that is produced in a life, or as it were, the byproduct of the seed planted and growing. God's fruit in a life is directly related to the vitality of the grace freely given. No observable spiritual fruit can mean only one thing: no spiritual life. We cannot produce spiritual fruit through our effort, yet many churched people have tried.

Like the plastic fruit used for home or office decoration or staging, perhaps you have experienced the fake fruit of a churched person and been turned off. When you try to experience what is fake, it leaves a bad taste in your mouth. But not so with real, luscious, flavorful, juicy, and fresh fruit. That kind bursts in your senses, leaving you with a longing for more. Same with the Spirit's fruit being grown in a life.

I hope at some level we understand that the involvement of the Holy Spirit, whom Jesus sent to us after His death, resurrection, and ascension, is His personal influence in us as we are experiencing grace-renewing dynamics in gospel 3D (delighting in Christ, distressing over continued sin, following Spirit's direction for living). And He is producing character and life qualities (inner affections and heart motivational changes, outwardly investing changes, and even upward or worship changes), or if you will, a "gospel influenced and influencing life."

In Galatians 5:22-23, Paul summarized in nine words the Holy Spirit's influence in the lives of those who have received the vital grace of Christ: love, joy, peace, patience, kindness, goodness, faithfulness, gentleness, and self-control. But they are not limited to this one passage. Throughout the New Testament, Jesus, Peter, John, James, Jude, and Paul expand and extend the life qualities we receive. They are normal, so not to have them growing in life is unusual.

As we abide (dwell, dine) in the True Vine (Jesus Christ), the Spirit produces fruit unto God (see Romans 7:4). However, as we have seen, it is possible that bad fruit can be produced from our former lives in the flesh. Like algae grows in the Dead Sea, you can grow something, it just is not a life worth enjoying.

When life by the Spirit is flowing through us, we are loving and deeply affectionate in our relationships. We love our spouses, children, family, neighbors, and coworkers in healthy and practical ways. We are able to defuse conflict when it arises. We have substantial relational healing, not living dependent upon their approval nor codependent for their reciprocity. When it comes to the nonbelieving watching world, what they see in churches are people who are expressing their love in meaningful ways with one another. They see service and forgiveness. In fact, forgiving others for their past or current offenses is an essential and remarkable quality of a heart that has been radically changed by grace alone.

Sam, a friend in one of my men's groups, related a conversation he had with a colleague at work. In a bit of jesting his colleague said to him, "You Christians are all brainwashed." Sam smiled and responded, "You wouldn't have liked me very much if we had met about ten years ago. I was harsh, impatient, and had a nasty mouth. I was cruel to people around me and unloving to my wife and two daughters. I was an unforgiving, selfish pig. My brain needed a good washing—and so did my eyes, my mouth, my hands, and my heart. The reason I work the way I do, care for all of you on my team, and have a loving home life is because in a really good way I did get 'brainwashed' by a loving Christ, alive and still working."

Churches that have a love-ability among its members demonstrate an engaging love that plastic fruit cannot mimic. It's more than taking a *"Hello, nice to have you this morning"* approach, as nice as that may be. It's about offering a helping hand. These church members are living out loud with a forgiveness of others who have hurt, offended, wounded, or wronged them deeply. They seek out justice and mercy for those who have been sinned against.

As the influence of the Spirit descends on our personal lives, we experience overflowing joy, thankfulness, and gratitude. We can deal with loss, grief, suffering, and hardship, not with a *Never let them see you cry* attitude, but with humble reliance that God is for us, not against us, and that He is always working. Even in the midst of my own pain, I have asked, "Where would I be without God?"

In the spheres where we work and serve, we are becoming peacemakers and are generous with our time, money, and resources for the well-being of others. We become more God's-Kingdom focused and less focused on our personal well-being, safety, affluence, and comfort.

Spiritually, we are in a continual discovery of a deep sense of gratitude and deeper love for God. Worshiping God moves us deeper into love for and faithfulness to Him. Self-control is that character quality of our hearts not simply a matter of our wills. It is the ability to focus life on the true treasure and subordinate all other affections or desires in order to have the best. That is an outpouring of the Spirit in the core.

A few years ago, a commercial for a deodorant proclaimed, "Never let them see you sweat." As a young believer, I was told that we should never let non-Christians see us sin because we'd be a bad testimony. So we hid our sins from others. We stayed away from "worldly" type things so we could say, *See? We are holy and good.* We pretended to have it all together, that we were above sin. The problem was we had a wrong understanding of sin and holiness. Most of our teachers saw it as a list of bad stuff and behaviors to avoid or as a bunch of religious stuff we were to do to make us good and acceptable to God.

But listen: the reality is the Spirit's fruit, the character of life, is you having the truest moral beauty, the deepest beauty.

Forget for a moment that you know anything about God, Jesus Christ, being "saved," or anything related to what you recognize as the Christian life. Now remember your sense of guilt. Remember the shame of a childhood trauma or the last time you did something you hoped would never be found out. Where would you go to find healing? Where would you turn to find forgiveness? Who could take away the deep sense of hiding shame? No matter how much you wish, declare it to a mirror, or how many times the counselor tells you, you cannot declare yourself not guilty or feel unashamed.

Many people I've known feel a deep-down nagging sense of guilt, shame, or both, and have plunged beneath a line of despair. For them, in order to make a "go of life," they simply stay busy. They subconsciously tell themselves, *Do not stop, keep moving, and do not pay any attention to the feelings of loss*. Some work hard, go to school, keep working on degrees. Others find a new movement or "righteous" cause to pour themselves into. Some tried church or a new religion and ended up with a new set of busyness and try-harder effort. You might be that person who not only has "been there done that, and have the T-shirt to prove it," you have a dozen of them. Many others drop so low that they escape by a climb into a bottle or rely on the numbness from a pill.

You see, what people need from you, what your son, daughter, neighbor, spouse need most from you isn't that you don't say bad words or live a naughty life. It is not your skill as a teacher or counselor. Your friends don't need you to fix them. No, what they need most is an attractiveness in your life. They need to see God, in His beauty, working in your life. And that is what we have formally called the fruit of the Spirit. They need to know a love that covers a multitude of sin and removes their guilt and shame. Your Spirit-influenced life is the shaping influence they desperately need.

However, the fruit, the Spirit-influenced life, is sometimes seen best in the midst of how you deal with failure, disappointment, or pain. Because we have rid ourselves of the delusion that we can handle suffering by relying on our own willpower and strength, they need to see that we have vital grace in the trenches of pain and sorrow.

When were people most attracted to Jesus? It was when He dealt with the people who had failed, the outcasts of society, and the people who were suffering. It was when He was in the throes of His own pain and loss; when He was harshly criticized, yet He did not revile back. That is true beauty. True wonder. True love.

God's glory is supremely His goodness—His beauty—and it is best seen now, through Him working in your life. This is the gospel influence and influencing life. When the gospel of grace is working in life, it is producing in you an attractiveness that others want to have. And when it is the Spirit producing in your life the love, joy, peace, patience, kindness, goodness, faithfulness, gentleness, and self-control (it is not fruits but fruit), it probably will be as much as a surprise to you as it is to others!

Spiritual Skills for Influencing Others

Every person who has had God supernaturally change them and has received a new identity in Christ (creatureship, kinship, and discipleship) has been given a spiritual gift or spiritual skill for serving and caring for others. As Paul explained, "We have different gifts, according to the grace given to each of us" (Romans 12:6).

Before we look at them, let me caution us about focusing on the skills or spiritual gifts as the greatest focus point. Too often we elevate the uber-gifted to a place of honor and fame the Lord did not intend, whether it is their speaking, singing, or leadership.

Which has more influence on others—character or skill? Obviously, we can look back over the past at the extremely gifted and skilled platform speakers or worship leaders who have been removed from those perches, and know their crash was not for lack of skill, but of character. Character trumps competency every day, and it will often cover skill deficiency. Most leadership failures are a result of poor or disqualifying character. Gifts or spiritual skills are important for our continued growth personally and in our churches, but they are to work in partnership with the Spirit's influence on our characters—as evidenced by our spiritual fruit. While skill competency can never make up for character deficiency, people with true life character are those who have the most significant and lasting influence on our lives.

In 1 Corinthians 12:1-7, Paul informed the Christians in Corinth, "Now about the gifts of the Spirit. . . . When you were pagans . . . you were influenced and led astray to mute idols. . . . There are different kinds of gifts, but the same Spirit distributes them. . . . Now to each one the manifestation of the Spirit is given for the common good." We are now to be influenced by the Spirit (as opposed to being under another controlling substance) as we utilize the Spirit's freely given unique gifts or skills.

I am calling them skills because in our culture that is how we view the ability of someone—they are skilled at their job. But when we think of them as the Bible calls them, gifts, we are reminded that they are supernaturally assigned to us by His graciousness. Whatever skill I have, God gifted me as an expression of His glory, for the benefit of others who bear His image, and I am to excel in the skill given to me. As Peter instructed believers in 1 Peter 4:10: "Each of you should use whatever gift you have received to serve others, as faithful stewards of God's grace in its various forms."

Many gifts or spiritual skills are listed in various Bible passages, but I will summarize them in three categories.

Speaking Skills

In the United States, Christian, varied religions, and secularists all put a high premium on communication skills, singing, or speaking gifts. In the secular pagan world, whether acting, singing, newscasting, or politicking, much is gained by the ability to speak well. In the church, the spiritual skill of teaching is given to some so they clearly and effectively can explain the gospel of grace in such a way that other Christians are able to understand it and apply it to life. Preaching or prophecy is given to some to proclaim Christ's saving grace in ways that disclose the mystery of the gospel to nonbelievers and also to build up believers in the grace of the gospel. Those with the skill of evangelizing lost people have a speaking gifting as do many pastor-shepherds. Maybe not all are great when speaking to large groups, but their ability to communicate to small groups or with their teenager is supernatural.

We also have contemporary songwriters and worship leaders who speak to us with "psalms, hymns, and songs from the Spirit" (Ephesians 5:19). Speaking gifts may be celebrated culturally, but for the Spirit influenced, they recognize it as a gift, not a natural talent to be used for selfish gain.

Serving Skills

We can see from Paul's list of spiritual skills in Romans 12 that he places "serving" in the number two slot on the list, between two speaking gifts. And then he adds other skills related to serving to fill out the list, such as encouraging (to come alongside and put courage back into someone), generously giving resources or money, leading (positively influencing others toward a desired goal), hospitality (making someone feel right at home when you wish they were), and serving others with hilarious demonstrations of mercy. More serving gifts exist than the platform skills of speaking or singing we usually celebrate.

If you have a serving skill (such as mercy or helps), you have been given it to assist in the worldwide Kingdom growth by maturing fellow followers or yet-to-be Christ followers in the land of amazing grace. Even though your gift may tend to not be as visible as speaking, be careful not to envy or feel inferior to those with different gifts or skills. The body needs hands, arms, eyes, ears, legs, and feet (see 1 Corinthians 12). He gave all those in twos but only gave one mouth!

Unseeable Skills

The Holy Spirit has equipped some people with skills that are typically unseen in this realm. Men and women whom God has granted a spiritual sixth sense (an awareness to a spiritual battle being waged in what is unseen to the human eye) and who intercede for God's intervention possess an exceedingly rare and valuable gift. Like the woman who serves in the background, not wanting to be known for her kind deeds of sacrifice, intercessors are typically using their prayer and miracle skills in their prayer chair or in small prayer cells. They enjoy extended times of worship and prayer and can actually become physically exhausted by the heavy lifting of prayer. With or without knowable results of their prayers, they continue on in believing prayer. It seems that Epaphras had the gift of intercession because Paul wrote that "he is always wrestling in prayer for you, that you may stand firm in the will of God, mature and fully assured" (Colossians 4:12).

Yes, we are called to serve others, to speak the truth in love, to give encouragement to one another, to give generous offerings to the

Lord and His Kingdom, and to practice mercy to others. We all, as we saw, have been given the means of growing in grace by prayer. But some of us are uniquely and specially gifted or skilled to love God and others by mastering our craft to increase God's grace.

The skills or gifts are supernatural. The Evil One knows that if you have natural ability or skills, that it isn't a supernatural gifting and so you do not have to rely on Christ. You can rely on yourself or something else. You end up thinking you really don't need grace (getting everything we need for nothing), at least not 100 percent. However, you have a significant skill for God's mission because the Holy Spirit has graciously provided it to you so that you can share with others for their spiritual health and common good.

Is God Just Using You?

Often we say, "God wants to use you" or encourage others with, "God is using you in such powerful ways." I know we mean it in a positive way, but don't you hate being used? At some point in life a friend points out to you, "She is just using you to get what she wants" or "He just used you for his own pleasure." Whether it is at work, home, or in a friendship, few people enjoy being "used" by someone. Really, who wants to be used?

We have to be careful in our talk about God wanting to use us that we do not misrepresent God to others. I have said and have been told, "God wants to use you for . . ." or "God is using you for good."

However, God—because He is not a single person/unit god in the universe, being completely and perfectly interdependent relationally, as Father, Son, and Spirit—did not make humans because He needed to use us or needed to be served by us. God is not a user.

God did not rescue you because He needed you to serve Him, and He did not rescue you to use you in any sense that provides Him with approval, security, or comfort. He is all glorious; who can add to His honor or make Him famous? He is all powerful; who can be His rival or threaten His secured Kingdom? He is all good and eternally loving; who can offer Him more comfort than His Presence can provide? Be humbled that He is complete in and of Himself and offers Himself to you.

He is glorified in and through us when we treasure Him with our love in worship and reliance, as well as when we love our neighbor as Christ loved us. He is not interested in using us for His personal gain, but He does ask for us to show up as a witness to who He is, all He's done, and all He is doing.

Can I Get a Witness?

I have been asked to be a witness on several different occasions. One was for an accident I saw happen right in front of me. All the others were at weddings, either as the minister or in attendance, witnessing the union of a man and woman in marriage. Witnesses tell only what they saw or experienced. Witnesses are not supposed to give commentary or add to what they saw.

Consider this witness who interacted with Jesus. One day Jesus met a man who had been born blind. Jesus mixed some mud in His hands and put it on the man's eyes, instructing him to go and wash it off in a pool nearby. When the man washed the mud off his face, he was healed. When his neighbours noticed him walking around gazing at the scenery, probably with lots of laughter, they stopped him and asked how it was that he was no longer blind. He told them a man named Jesus did it.

The religious leaders got involved because the healing broke their Sabbath rule. When they interrogated the formerly blind man, they wanted to use him in order to accuse Jesus of being a sinner for breaking their rules. They even tried to use the man's parents for their ends. The now joy-filled and 20/20-seeing man looked at them face to face for the first time in his life and answered their questions with the now-famous saying, "One thing I do know. I was blind but now I see!" (John 9:25). He was just a first-hand witness to the miracle-performing Jesus Christ.

Since the catastrophe in the garden, God is on a mission to rescue and reconcile men, women, boys, and girls who are enslaved by the curse of death. He has you for His mission and, by His Spirit, He is shaping you as well as providing the necessary skills to join Him on His mission. All of us on mission are first and foremost witnesses of a living, risen Savior (see Acts 1:8).

Jesus Himself, who after His resurrection showed them His hands and feet, proving He once was dead but was now alive, began with Moses and all the Prophets, and "explained to them what was said in all the Scriptures concerning himself" (Luke 24:27). He told them, "'Everything must be fulfilled that is written about me in the Law of Moses, the Prophets and the Psalms.' Then he opened their minds so they could understand the Scriptures" (Luke 24:44-45).

Notice, Jesus didn't offer them a fill-in-the-blank version of life. He gave them the gospel story, from beginning to end. He said that He had to die and on third day be raised to life and that now repentance and forgiveness of sins would be offered to all the nations. He said in a sense, "You are characters in the gospel story." Why? Because, "*You are witnesses* of these things [the resurrection—the greatest event in the history of the world]. I am going to send [the Spirit]" to be in you and empower you" (Luke 24:48-49, emphasis added).

One of ways the Spirit gives an outpouring of the grace of God is when we go on the mission God is on. Jesus also told the disciples that when they were asked about their hope in their newfound faith in Him, the Holy Spirit would "teach you at that time what you should say" (Luke 12:12).

We should always be prepared to give an answer to anyone who asks for the reason we have hope, as Peter encouraged us in 1 Peter 3:15. What will the Spirit tell you is the hope? Peter's pen flowed directly to the grace given through the death and resurrection of Christ: "Christ also suffered once for sins . . . to bring you to God. He was put to death in the body but made alive in the Spirit" (1 Peter 3:18). It is the vital grace of God that we are all to be a witness to. We can testify that God's loving grace through a living, risen Savior is true and He is able to save anyone who relies on Him. He gave you the Spirit, His fruit, and His skill.

Influencing Others by Specific Role

We have become a therapeutic culture. When friends are having personal struggles, many generally ask, "Have you seen a counselor or therapist for that?" Because some of us are overly protective of our personal space, we are unwilling to spend the time and ability to care for someone else's spiritual development or we don't want to intrude on another's private life, so we have a form of Christianity that is privatized to Sunday mornings or impersonal online church. Some of us simply do not feel qualified to invest in others with our spiritual skill set.

"Am I my brother's keeper?" (Genesis 4:9) was Cain's answer when God asked him the whereabouts of his brother Abel. God knew what had happened, so the question was to draw Cain out of hiding. Of course, the implied answer was "Yes, you are your brother's keeper." You are to love your neighbor as yourself, or if you are a Christian, as Christ loved you.

The apostle Peter wrote, "Above all, love each other deeply, because love covers over a multitude of sins. . . . Each of you should use whatever gift you have received to serve others, as faithful stewards of God's grace in its various forms" (1 Peter 4:8, 10).

I remind you of Paul's summary of it all in 2 Corinthians 5:15, that "those who live [because of Jesus' substitutionary death for them] should no longer live for themselves but for him who died for them and was raised again."

We are to be a living sacrifice. To die daily to our self-reliance, self-saving strategies, and our selfish-oriented comfort. We are to deny ourselves and pick up a cross to follow Christ in loving brothers and sisters. Now we are dying to live! I want to invite you to a new view and return to a basic reality: let the gospel of grace do its work in the simplicity of what God invited you to do in being a witness to a real, living Christ inside you, by being your brother's keeper, as it were, using the spiritual skill He gave you, in a role He designed.

This is an invitation to make vital grace move beyond the personal changes we tend to focus on and enlarge it to the movement God is on. You have been graced by friends, teachers, mentors, coaches, and disciplers who influence you, and now, for that grace to grow deeper, you are to allow grace to flow through your life into the lives of others, inside and outside of the Christian faith. That is a way it will become vital grace in your life.

I ask you to explore one of the four potential roles in which to involve yourself. These roles come through the Spirit's work in your sphere of influence, whether in family life, church, business, media, politics, arts, social services, medicine, or education. I know you can pursue this role since the Spirit is changing your character (spiritual fruit) and has graciously given you a Spirit skill to be a witness that Jesus Christ is alive and able to do more than we can imagine (see Ephesians 3:20). Yes, it will be messy. You may feel safer in the learner position, sitting in someone else's living room, or taking a class or seminar, but that limits what grace is meant to do. Vital grace is to be shared through making other disciples who embrace vital grace, by mentoring a younger leader or couple, by engaging God and His Kingdom mission as a prayer catalyst with others, or by gospel coaching another Christian in his or her unique job or capacity. When you influence one person, your influence is multiplied into others' lives in their spheres, such as a spouse, children, friends, coworkers, neighbors, and city. Let's look at these four roles.

Disciple-Maker

Disciple-making in relationship with others is a major call to the church (see Matthew 28:16-20) that was inaugurated in the call of Abraham to have God's grace be a blessing to the nations.

We have made disciple-making more complex than it should be. A disciple of Jesus is someone who has repented and continues to confess of their sinful, self-saving strategies, believed and continues to believe that Christ is the only Savior, and is following after Him in an ongoing obedient life of worship, community, and mission. Disciple-making then is not simply a teaching class of information download. It is continually developing one another in life in community, through applying the gospel 3D. It is a grace-shaped life shaping other lives.

Part of your identity, as we looked at in chapter six, is that you are a disciple and being discipled by the Holy Spirit now.

As a disciple-maker, you aim for the heart, because vital grace always deals at the heart, or the deep motivational structures of what people are really living for. If disciple-making does not get to the heart, it will not produce change transformation into the likeness of the True Man—Jesus Christ. You do not have to be an expert in Christianity to be a disciple-maker; you just need to be a disciple who invites others into a community of fellow followers.

If you are a parent, one of your most important investments in the life of your child is to disciple them through prayer, teaching God's love and God's warnings, correcting them, and living out of Spirit's fruit, so they want to love God and follow Christ in their life and career.

We will change our world through ongoing, engaging, and loving men and women who courageously assume the role of disciple-makers in their homes, businesses, schools, and churches.

Gospel Mentor

The second role to consider is a gospel mentor. Disciple-making is best done in a small community of three or four people, while mentoring is better done one-on-one or one-on-two. Mentors can dramatically change a life. Along the journey called life, they come alongside to provide the navigation Christians need for living engaged in a spiritual war in our broken down, pain-filled, runaway world. Mentoring is like disciple-making and coaching, but is not the same kind of relationship.

Gospel mentoring is a trusting relationship between an experienced mentor and maturing mentoree that involves engaging life-on-life conversations with grace-renewing dynamics, aimed to empower holistically the relational, personal, missional, and spiritual life of the mentoree. It is a highly relational experience in which one person significantly contributes to the holistic development or empowerment of a maturing person. It is showing someone how to be someone. And because we mentor by the grace dynamic, it means we can lead not simply from our strengths and successes, but also from our weaknesses and failures. I have a sign in my office that reads, "Good judgment comes from experience. And experience, well, that comes from poor judgment." Gospel mentors engaging with maturing men and women have a unique value to change the world.

Prayer Catalysts

What does believing in vital grace have to do with praying? Being disconnected from vital grace and relying on our own efforts, abilities, and protection disconnects us from the God of all grace. When we view our relationship with God as transactional—we do our part and He makes up for the difference that we cannot accomplish—then we tend to rely on our own work most of the time. We pray when we get in over our heads; that is, when we get into situations we can't manage. Even when we do pray, it is really giving God advice on how to accomplish our plan. Christianity then becomes simply about us bettering our personal selves, it becomes predictably programmed.

The false belief is God is there to make us happy, so the Christian life becomes primarily about personal change not about God and His Kingdom displayed on earth. Prayer, then, becomes a function of our wish lists for God to fulfill. And when He doesn't respond, we quit. Our prayerlessness becomes a thief and a robber of what we have in Christ.

Prayer catalysts have come to the wonder of a relationship with God that exists only by His kindness of amazing grace—that He has done everything and given it freely, not because of any efforts or works—and they treasure prayer for the friendship it offers. As Jesus said to His disciples:

> I no longer call you servants, because a servant does not know his master's business. Instead, I have called you friends, for everything that I learned from my Father I have made known to you. You did not choose me, but I chose you and appointed you so that you might go and bear fruit—fruit that will last—and so that whatever you ask in my name the Father will give you. (John 15:15-16)

As I mentioned in the spiritual skill section, some Christians have the gift of intercession. They are men and women who connect to God in prayer, fasting, and worship in Kingdom-shaping ways. Paul, who had a speaking gift, solicited the prayer catalysts to ask God to give him the ability to use his speaking gift fearlessly and for God's protection from evil men. If you are one of those people and you haven't started a prayer cell, now that grace has been reengaged in your life, I encourage you to start prayer friendships with other believers for community Kingdom-centered prayer, because we are a prayerless church.

Gospel Coaches

Coaching is a specialty role in the church. Not everyone can coach, but gospel coaching is the single most important ingredient in the health and sustainability of a leader.

Who is often the most under-resourced person in the church or ministry? Who gets the least amount of support and attention? Some of the chief complaints of many leaders are that they feel uncared for and under-appreciated. They don't know if they are doing a good job, not receiving feedback or encouragement. Coaching is one of the key solutions to providing the resource needed for leaders and provides the intentional gospel conversation for their relational, personal, missional, and spiritual lives.

A mentor of mine, Dr. J. Allen Thompson, told me, "Coaching is developing a supportive relationship with the coachee that leads to continual gospel renewal and character deepening, that focuses on the realities of cultural life, and results in the improvement of skills and performance by a form of instructions that enables the coachee to build awareness and responsibility."

I studied and pioneered gospel coaching nearly fifteen years ago. I have had the privilege of coaching leaders, training others in gospel coaching, and am president of a ministry that deploys gospel coaches globally. Reproducing leaders is the most important task of any person with influence. When you raise up and empower leaders through gospel coaching, you make a positive impact on yourself, your organization, your generation, and the next generation.

Agents of Grace

What is the aim of vital grace? It is God's glory in the rescue of His people and renewal of all things on this runaway planet. We have been given grace to do "good works." Our good works are not to be seen as only in a spiritual sense by grace growing and shaping our character. Vital grace moves us into mission as agents of His ongoing grace being offered to Christians and not-yet Christians. Grace given as our inheritance is mysteriously enlarged when in our hearts we are discipling, mentoring, praying, or coaching as a grace-giving influencer.

Now I suspect you may be thinking, *You do not know the things I've done. You don't know my past and how awful it has been.* True. I do not know. God never asks us to dismiss the past. We are not to neglect or deny the pain we received or caused in our past. One misquoted passage to the hurting and guilty is "Forgetting what is behind . . . I press on" (Philippians 3:13-14). God's grace does not free us from looking at the past, rather it gives us the courage we need to look at it, repent and confess of anything we have done to cause the ruin, face any shame we have assumed, and work out the renewing dynamics of grace with courage and hope.

While it is true you cannot change your past, your past guilt and shame have been forgiven and covered, and the power of vital grace will change the future of where that past was going to take you. You are still an agent of grace. As you recover the grand cosmic scope of salvation, it will move you out of the narrowness and anxiety of self-preoccupation into being a gospel influencer.

As new creatures granted the grace of God in Christ, we are to share that grace with others through relationships, despite our discomfort, insecurities, or fear of disapproval. Or I should say, we get to live by faith in a new life of comfort, security, and approval in Christ and His Spirit communing with us moment by moment.

Christ is full of grace, and those who know Him get showered with grace when being on mission. As the apostle John wrote, "Out of his fullness we have all received grace in place of grace already given" (John 1:16). His grace, demonstrated in His being "on mission" of mercy, is multiplied to us who go on mission. To those who have been given much (everything for us), much will be expected (see Luke 12:48). Grace flows into mission not into a sea of deadness.

There is an amazing connection between the opening backstory in the first book of the Bible and the last book. We found in the backstory that God created heaven and earth. The last book, Revelation, paints a glorious future of a recreated, renewed heaven and earth. The backstory described the painful action of rebellion, our parents in hiding, cursed out of their garden, kept from the tree of life, as well as our lost, ruined paradise. The last book invites us to see God with us, welcomed to the tree of life, and to experience the nations streaming into the new city.

The sixty-six books in the Bible close the entire scope of God's revelation to us with these words: "The grace of the Lord Jesus be with God's people. Amen" (Revelation 22:21). Vital grace connects us to the God of all grace and compels us to see that we are part of a new cosmic, global Kingdom, which will be what restores all things because our gracious King will return. God will renew His presence and dwell with us, wiping away every tear, suffering, and sadness, ending disease and death. He will make all things new! It began by God giving everything for nothing and will end with an ending that never ends, in grace being with God's people.

Vital GRACE

Download Your FREE LABS

In order for us to get the Gospel of Grace to grab us, to work it down into the way we believe — to affect our thinking and into the practice of Love (enjoying life with God and others), so we are being influenced by grace and influencing others with grace — we need to develop the skill and art of "Vital Grace" conversations.

These FREE six labs are to provide a transferable experience of pressing the Grace of God we received into patterns of life.

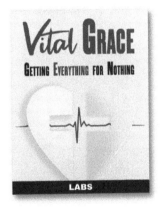

Notes

Chapter One: The Vitality of Grace

1 John Henry Sammis, "Trust and Obey," 1887, public domain.

2 Philip Yancey, *What's So Amazing About Grace* (Grand Rapids, MI: Zondervan, 1997), 208.

3 Helmut Lehmann, ed., *Luther's Works*, ed. and trans. John Doberstein (Philadelphia: Fortress, 1966), 284–85.

4 John Piper, *God Is the Gospel: Meditations on God's Love as the Gift of Himself* (Wheaton, IL: Crossway, 2005), 167.

5 Werner Mischke, *The Global Gospel: Achieving Missional Impact in Our Multicultural World,* (Scottsdale, AZ: Mission One, 2015), 64–65.

6 Dan Allender and Tremper Longman III, *The Cry of the Soul: How Our Deepest Emotions Reveal Our Deepest Questions about God* (Colorado Springs, CO: NavPress, 1994), 196.

7 Bob Bennett, "A Song About Baseball," EMI Christian Music Group (Straightway Music), 1982.

8 David Powlison, *Seeing with New Eyes: Counseling and the Human Condition Through the Lens of Scripture* (Philipsburg, NJ: P&R Publishing, 2003), 170.

9 C. S. Lewis, *Mere Christianity* (San Francisco: HarperOne, 1952, 1980), 142.

10 Richard Lovelace, *Dynamics of Spiritual Life: An Evangelical Theology of Renewal* (Downers Grove, IL: InterVarsity, 1979), 211–12.

Chapter Two: Understanding the Backstory of Grace

1 Steven Curtis Chapman, *Where We Belong*, 1992 lyrics, © BMG Rights Management.

2 Richard Dawkins, *The God Delusion* (Boston: Houghton Mifflin, 2006), 51.

3 Francis Schaeffer, *True Spirituality* (Wheaton, IL: Tyndale, 1971), 88.

4 Larry Crabb, *Inside Out* (Colorado Springs, CO: NavPress, 1988), 72.

5 C. John Collins, *Did Adam and Eve Really Exist?: Who They Were and Why You Should Care* (Wheaton, IL: Crossway, 2011), 15.

6 C. S. Lewis, *Mere Christianity* (New York: Macmillan, 1952), 53–54.

7 *Finding Your Roots*, season 6, episode 4: "This Land Is My Land," January 14, 2020, https://www.pbs.org/video/ancestors-freed-slavery-nfwc2j/.

Chapter Three: Our Vital Rescue

1 Christopher J. H. Wright, *The Mission of God's People: A Biblical Theology of the Church's Mission* (Grand Rapids, MI: Zondervan, 2010), 66.

2 Matt Rosenberg, "Largest Cities Throughout History," ThoughtCo, November 4, 2019, https://www.thoughtco.com/largest-cities-throughout-history-4068071.

3 Christopher J. H. Wright, *Knowing Jesus Through the Old Testament* (Downers Grove, IL: InterVarsity, 1992), 4.

4 Rich Mullins and David Strasser, "Sometimes By Step," Copyright © 1992, Edward Grant, Inc., Kid Brothers of St. Frank's Publishing.

5 Steve Brown, *Three Free Sins: God's Not Mad at You* (New York: Howard Books, 2012), 121.

6 J. I. Packer, *Knowing God* (Downers Grove, IL: InterVarsity, 1973), 186.

7 Tim Keller, *Counterfeit Gods: The Empty Promises of Money, Sex, and Power, and the Only Hope that Matters* (New York: Dutto Adult, 2009), 10.

8 Keller, *Counterfeit Gods,* 18.

9 Charles Wesley, "And Can It Be," 1738, public domain.

Chapter Four: Ball and Chain: The Power of Your Former Life

1 Scott Thomas and Tom Wood, *Gospel Coach: Shepherding Leaders to Glorify God* (Grand Rapids, MI: Zondervan, 2012), 85.

2 Martin Lloyd-Jones, *Life in Christ: Studies in 1 John* (Wheaton, IL: Crossway, 2002), 725.

3 *The Heidelberg Catechism*, Question/Answer 95, accessed September 6, 2021, https://www.crcna.org/welcome/beliefs/confessions/heidelberg-catechism.

4 Richard Keyes, "The Idol Factory," in *No God But God: Breaking with the Idols of Our Age,* Os Guinness and John Seel, eds. (Chicago: Moody, 1995), 31–33.

5 Thomas and Wood, *Gospel Coach,* 85–86.

6 As quoted in Jerry Newcombe, "The Thunderstorm that Changed Martin Luther's Life," *The Christian Post*, November 4, 2017, https://www.christianpost.com/news/the-thunderstorm-that-changed-martin-luthers-life.html.

7 Thomas Chalmers, *Expulsive Power of a Higher Affection*, my paraphrase.

8 Romans 6:15-17 Commentary, Precept Austin, January 24, 2020, https://www.preceptaustin.org/romans_615-20.

9 Jamie Ducharme, "More Millennials Are Dying 'Deaths of Despair,' as Overdose and Suicide Rates Climb," Time, June 13, 2019, https://time.com/5606411/millennials-deaths-of-despair/.

10 Olga Khazan, "The Millennial Mental-Health Crisis, *The Atlantic*, June 11, 2020, https://www.theatlantic.com/health/archive/2020/06/why-suicide-rates-among-millennials-are-rising/612943/.

11 *The Lord of the Rings: The Fellowship of the Ring*, 2001, directed by Peter Jackson, New Line Cinema.

Chapter Five: What Is True Spirituality?

1 Francis Schaeffer, *True Spirituality* (Wheaton, IL: Tyndale, 1971), 87.

2 John Piper, *God's Passion for His Glory: Living the Vision of Jonathan Edwards* (Wheaton, IL: Crossway, 1998), 41.

3 Michael Horton, *The Christian Faith: A Systematic Theology for Pilgrims on the Way* (Grand Rapids, MI: Zondervan, 2011), 405.

4 Heidelberg Catechism, Question #26, "God the Father," accessed September 6, 2021, https://www.crcna.org/welcome/beliefs/confessions/heidelberg-catechism.

5 Martin Luther, *Commentary on Galatians,* fourth edition (Grand Rapids, MI: Zondervan, nd), 20.

6 C. S. Lewis, *The Weight of Glory* (Grand Rapids, MI: Eerdmans, 1949), 38.

7 Stephen Smallman, *The Walk: Steps for New and Renewed Followers of Jesus* (Phillipsburg, NJ: P& R Publishing, 2009), 26. Emphasis added.

8 Elvina M. Hall, "Jesus Paid It All," copyright ©1865, public domain.

9 Robert Robinson, "Come Thou Fount," copyright ©1758, public domain.

10 Steve Brown, "Steve's Devotional—We Owe Love . . . Even WhenTreated Like Dirt," Key Life, March 2, 2020, **Vital Grace 5.25 x 8 inch (13.34 x 20.32 cm) 12-23-21.doc**https://www.keylife.org/articles/steves-devotional-we-owe-loveeven-when-treated-like-dirt/.

11 *Book of Common Prayer,* 1662.

Chapter Six: Amazing Grace Land

1 Frances Schaeffer, *True Spirituality* (Wheaton, IL: Tyndale, 1971), 86–87.

2 Martin Luther, *Luther's Works,* vol. 54, ed. Theodore G. Tappert (Minneapolis, MN: Fortress Press, 1967), 37.

3 Steve Childers, *True Spirituality*, unpublished.

4 Paul David Tripp, "Counseling Toward Repentance," (www.BuildingChurchLeaders.com, Christianity Today International, Carol Stream, IL) 2010), 6.

5 Steve Brown, *Born Free: How to Find Radical Freedom and Infectious Joy in an Authentic Faith* (Grand Rapids, MI: Baker, 1993), 157.

6 Schaeffer, *True Spirituality*, 89.

7 A. W. Tozer, *The Pursuit of God* (Bloomington, MN: Bethany, 2013), 10.

8 Heidelberg Catechism, 1563, Question & Answer #1, accessed September 6, 2021, https://www.crcna.org/welcome/beliefs/confessions/heidelberg-catechism.

9 *Braveheart*, screenplay written by Randall Wallace. Produced by Icon Productions and The Ladd Company, 1995.

10 Richard Lovelace, *Dynamics of Spiritual Life* (Downers Grove, IL: InterVarsity, 1979), 90.

11 C. S. Lewis, *Letters of C. S. Lewis* (C. S. Lewis Pte. Ltd. and W. H. Lewis, 1966, 1988, https://www.biblegateway.com/devotionals/cs-lewis-daily/2018/04/13.

12 Thomas Chalmers, "The Expulsive Power of a Higher Affection," sermon given 1830, public domain.

Chapter Seven: Graced Again and Again and Again . . .

1 Ann Voskamp, *One Thousand Gifts: A Dare to Live Fully Right Where You Are* (Grand Rapids, MI: Zondervan, 2010), 17. Emphasis in the original.

2 Albert M. Wolters, *Creation Regained: Biblical Basics for a Reformational Worldview* (Grand Rapids, MI: Eerdmans, 2005), 125.

3 "Signs of Decline and Hope Among Key Metrics of Faith," Barna: State of the Church, 2020, accessed December 17, 20212, https://www.barna.com/research/changing-state-of-the-church/.

4 John Smed, *Prayer Revolution: Rebuilding Church and City Through Prayer* (Chicago: Moody, 2020), 37–38.

5 "Public Worship of the Lord's Day. Scripture Reading and Preaching," History of the Christian Church, accessed December 17, 2021, https://ccel.org/ccel/schaff/hcc3/hcc3.iii.x.xvii.html.

6 Martin Luther, *Luther's Commentary of Galatians,* trans. Theodore Gradebner, fourth ed. (Grand Rapids, MI: Zondervan, nd), 159.

7 J. I. Packer, *God's Plans for You* (Wheaton, IL: Crossway Books, 2001), np.

Chapter Eight: From Influenced to Influencing

1 Christopher Wright, *The Mission of God's People* (Grand Rapids, MI: Zondervan, 2010), 46.

About the Author

Tom Wood is president of CMM, Inc. (Church Multiplication Ministries) and pioneer of Gospel Coaching. He earned his doctorate in coaching and has been coaching leaders for more than fourteen years. CMM trains others to be gospel coaches and consults with churches for grace renewing vitality. He is the author of *Gospelling Life Together*, *Church Planter Field Manual*, and coauthor of *Gospel Coach*. He and his wife, Rachel, live in greater Atlanta, Georgia. They have three daughters, two sons-in-law, and four grandchildren.

Information on CMM

Church Multiplication Ministries (CMM) innovatively connects leaders and churches with vital grace dynamics, so they are both gospel influenced and gospel influencers throughout the world. CMM is a donor-supported ministry that provides gospel coaching, vital grace workshops, church health assessments, and gospel-rich resources. We are empowering leaders to multiply the gospel in their spheres of influence.

For information about Church Multiplication Ministries, contact us at www.cmmnet.org.